CORACLES
OF THE WORLD

Coracles of the World

Peter Badge

First published in 2009

© Peter Badge/Gwasg Carreg Gwalch 2009

Published with the financial support
of the Welsh Books Council.

ISBN: 978-1-84527-255-5

Cover design: Sian Parri

Published by Gwasg Carreg Gwalch,
12 Iard yr Orsaf, Llanrwst, Wales LL26 0EH
tel: 01492 624031
fax: 01492 641502
email: books@carreg-gwalch.com
website: www.carreg-gwalch.com

To Mary,
my most supportive and patient wife,
with deep gratitude.
Without her encouragement
this book would not have seen the light of day.

Contents

Foreword

This book is the product of a lifetime's fascination with coracles and the culmination of three decades of scholarly and original research on the part of the author. No-one is better qualified to write on the subject than Peter Badge. Not only has he an unsurpassed knowledge of coracles and related craft throughout the world, but he is also an experienced and highly skilled coracle-maker and handler. As the founder and driving force behind the Coracle Society he has also done more than anyone to popularise coracling as a leisure activity. His own fine collection of coracles, which includes examples of virtually every known type, is on public display at various venues around the UK. He has also been a tireless campaigner on behalf of the rights of the few remaining Welsh coracle-fishermen to continue to practice their ancient craft.

This book builds on a long and honourable tradition. During the 1930s and 1940s, the scientist and ethnologist James Hornell published extensively on coracles and allied craft found in the various parts of the world. Later in the 1970s J Geraint Jenkins produced an equally authoritative account of the coracles of England and Wales. Much new information has come to light in the intervening thirty years, however, and interest in coracles has burgeoned beyond all expectation. The author performs a great service in bringing together all this new knowledge and disseminating it to the wider public.

The author combines the strengths of both Hornell and Jenkins and indeed the book is an exemplar of ethnological research, combining detailed knowledge of the archival and historical sources with extensive fieldwork and in-depth practical experience of coracle-making and handling. This is one of the book's great strengths, as the author's practical experience provides him with a level of insight which cannot be achieved by academic study alone. When, therefore, he assesses historical accounts of coracle construction or use he does so with the authority of someone who has actually built and handled such craft with his own hands. This extensive practical knowledge has also enabled him to venture into the realms of experimental archaeology by reconstructing long-disappeared coracle types, thereby adding greatly to the sum of our knowledge.

Naturally the author pays the greatest attention to the coracles of the British Isles, of which he has an unrivalled knowledge. Indeed his assiduous research has led to the discovery of some hitherto unrecorded coracle types. He also widens our horizons by placing coracles in their international context, revealing a story which will no doubt surprise those readers who think of coracles as being uniquely Welsh. He begins his study in North America with the Native American bull boat, perhaps the most primitive of the entire genre, but also possibly the best documented when it was in use as an everyday craft. Intriguingly for us in Wales, the similarity between the bull boat and the coracle was used by some as evidence in support of the Madog legend and of the existence of a tribe of Welsh-speaking Indians. Sadly this does not stand up to the author's forensic scrutiny! Equally fascinating are his detailed accounts of the coracle-like craft found in Iraq, India, Tibet and Vietnam, where they remain in daily use. Again much of this information draws on his own first hand experience of fieldwork in those areas.

Like Jenkins before him, Peter Badge owes much of his knowledge to many happy hours spent in conversation with the few remaining traditional coracle-makers. He acknowledges his debt to, and pays homage to, some remarkable individuals such as Eustace Rogers of Ironbridge, John E Davies of Shrewsbury and Bernard Thomas of Llechryd, who provided him with a wealth of information on a now disappeared way of life. These larger-than-life characters ensured, single-handedly in some cases, the survival of the tradition in their own localities: individuals who the Japanese would most certainly have classed as 'Living Treasures'!

The book also brings the story of the coracle up to the present day and chronicles the remarkable flowering of interest in coracling as a leisure activity over the past two decades. The Coracle Society, founded in 1991, played a crucial part in this process, inspiring a whole new generation of enthusiasts to take an interest in the craft. Coracle-making classes now flourish in many parts of the country, and coracles are now to be seen on the unlikeliest of rivers, canals and lakes. A craft which faced extinction when it first sparked the author's enthusiasm would now appear to have a bright and secure future.

It is a great privilege to have been asked to write the foreword to this book and to record the great debt students of traditional life owe the author. With typical modesty and generosity Peter pays fulsome tribute to James Hornell and J Geraint Jenkins – he can be assured that through this book he himself has emerged as their worthy successor.

John Williams-Davies
St Fagans

Introduction

My intense love of, and interest in, coracles was conceived when, as a schoolboy in north Wales in the 1940s, I saw an upper Dee coracle being used in the Llangollen area. The image of an angler fishing from a coracle being propelled by a coracle-handler has never left me. My interest remained dormant, however, until it was revived in 1981, when my wife Mary had a Teifi coracle made for me by Bernard Thomas of Llechryd, for my fiftieth birthday. Bernard took her to the Teifi where he showed her how to use it – she passed the knowledge on to me.

At the same time, coincidentally, Mary's sister was living in Shropshire, as a consequence of which I met two English traditional coraclemen. They were Eustace Rogers of Ironbridge and John E. Davies of Shrewsbury. Eustace made me an Ironbridge coracle and a hide coracle, and, over the years, gave me a priceless amount of information concerning coracle usage on the English Severn.

John not only made me a Shrewsbury coracle, but also a number of replicas of Welsh craft which were no longer made or used. These included the hitherto unknown Dwyryd coracle, which he discovered at the Isle, Bicton, near Shrewsbury. I was privileged to know John's father Jack, his uncle Fred, and his sons Mark and John, all of whom were skilled coracle-handlers. What is unusual about this stretch of the Severn is the fact that due to the formation of the river only the width of an average field separates the embarkation and disembarkation points of a lengthy river journey (approximately five miles). Normally when making such a journey in a coracle one would have had to walk five miles from beginning to end, or be collected from the finish. I was fortunate in having made several journeys on this stretch of the Severn with the Davies family. During these voyages I learnt how to handle a coracle and absorbed a lot of information about the traditional way of life of Shrewsbury coraclemen, particularly from John's father Jack.

Over the next twenty-seven years coracles were made for me by Raymond Rees of Carmarthen, Ronald Davies of Cenarth, Gerwyn Lewis of St Clears, Alan Grove of Kidderminster, and Andrew McGonagle of Owey Island, Donegal. I also acquired coracles from

India and Vietnam, where I saw them being made and used. I collaborated, too, with distinguished members of the Basket Makers' Association in the making of replica Boyne and Spey coracle-style curraghs.

In the 1980s the Welsh Folk Museum (as it was then known – now the Museum of Welsh Life) had the largest collection of coracles in Great Britain, so inevitably I visited it. There, it was my good fortune to meet Dr J. Geraint Jenkins, the highly respected author of a number of books on all aspects of rural life including coracles, and his very able deputy, John Williams-Davies. We shared a common concern at the all-too-obvious decline in the use and manufacture of coracles. We decided that the most practical way in which we could support the dwindling number of coraclemen was to form a Coracle Society. We duly did this, having enlisted the support of a group of like-minded people including the directors of the Greenwood Trust in Ironbridge, the Exeter Maritime Museum, and the Curator of the Bewdley Museum, who pioneered coracle-making courses with the Greenwood Trust. The first President was Geraint Jenkins, the Secretary John Williams-Davies, the Treasurer Jane Fogg of Bewdley Museum, and I was the Chairman.

I had by then given a number of my coracles to Martin Fowler, the director of the National Coracle Centre at Cenarth, who had built the Centre without the assistance of any outside body. It was fitting that following the formal opening of the Centre by Earl Lloyd-George on 21 June 1991, the inaugural meeting of the Coracle Society was held there, followed by a regatta nearby on the Teifi, on which were to be seen all the traditional coracle-makers of west Wales.

Over the years I succeeded Geraint as President; my successor as Chairman was Peter Faulkner, then of Leintwardine, who created the Teme coracle, in which he made many epic journeys as well as becoming a prolific coracle-builder, handler and exhibitor. In turn, Peter was followed into office by Conwy Richards of Kings Lynn, another builder of many different types of coracle, and the creator of a very busy website that has provided a vast amount of information to people all over the world.

The Society has three objectives, namely:

1. to assist in the preservation of the existing coracle way of life
2. to seek to revive interest in coracles in areas which had, but no longer have, such a heritage
3. to promote an interest in coracles in areas where they have not ever been made or used.

I will return to the reasons for the decline in traditional coracle usage in my final chapter, but suffice it to say that the Society has supported the Tywi coracle netsmen in their recent difficulties and has held coracle events in Welshpool and Bewdley in an attempt to rekindle their lost heritage. What is particularly heartening is the number of people attending the coracle-making courses at the Greenwood Trust, and the number of people in East Anglia who are now making and using coracles, some even in the traditional way.

Whilst the traditional use of coracles has been greatly diminished, there has been a considerable upsurge in the making of coracles for decorative and leisure purposes. It is suggested that the reason for this rise is to be found in the relative ease and cheapness of construction, together with the fact that a coracle can be carried in the average hatchback car without difficulty. There is no doubt that the excellent coracle-making courses provided by the Greenwood Trust in Shropshire have acted as a considerable stimulus in the making and using of coracles since the 1980s. It is suggested also that the emergence of the Coracle Society in 1990 has contributed considerably to the current interest in coracles.

For all these reasons it was felt that the time was ripe for another in-depth look at the coracles and similar craft of the world.

The very small amount of reliable written information concerning the coracle family makes it virtually impossible to be completely sure when they originated. A good example of this is to be found in the hypothesis of Professor T. Watkins[1] that grave 2 in the Early Bronze Age cemetery at Barns Farm, Dalgetty, Fife, contained a hide-boat burial, which was subsequently described by a former Professor of Maritime Archaeology at the University of Oxford, Sean McGrail, as 'meagre ...[and that] the direct evidence for Hide Boats in the Bronze Age in north west Europe is somewhat slight'.[2]

Another difficulty is distinguishing between coracles and curraghs in general descriptions. For instance, in *The Marsh Arabs* (1964), the highly respected explorer Wilfred Thesiger described a 'Zaima', which he saw on a branch of the Euphrates, as 'an interesting type of coracle', whereas its dimensions clearly show it to have been more akin to a curragh than a coracle.

Copious references to hide-covered boats exist as far back as 49 BC, as in James Hornell's *British Coracles and Irish Curraghs*, but again it is not clear whether the description relates to coracles or curraghs. Professor McGrail is of the opinion that craft having the characteristics of coracles could have been made as early as the Upper Palaeolithic period, the necessary skills by then being present.

Reference to coracles can be found in early Welsh literature, and in the works of the late James Hornell Esq, FLS, FRAI, and the previously mentioned Dr. J. Geraint Jenkins. Hornell and Jenkins, however, differ as to whether the appropriate descriptions refer to coracle or curragh-type crafts, Hornell inclining to the former, and Jenkins the latter. Be that as it may, clear evidence of the existence of coracles can be found in the *Gododdin*, a poem of Aneirin which can be dated to the seventh century: the following passage appears in Jenkins seminal work, *Nets and Coracles*: 'Ef lledi bysc yng corwc' [*he would kill fish in his coracle*].

In 1946, James Hornell, who had been active in the fields of fisheries and marine biology, and who had held important posts in the British empire, wrote his seminal work, *Water Transport: origins and early evolution*, which included an extensive section on coracles and allied craft of the word. Before this, however, he had written a series of articles which were reproduced in book form by the Society for Nautical Research in 1938, under the title *British Coracles and Irish Curraghs (with a note on the Quffah of Iraq)*. In his introduction to this book, Sir Geoffrey Callender, a former director of the National Maritime Museum, pointed out that it was 'somewhat strange that, until Mr Hornell devoted his attention to the subject, no-one had published any connected account of the fascinating and historically significant career of the wickerwork craft'.

As part of a wider scheme for the survey of coastal and river craft of Great Britain and Ireland whose futures were increasingly uncertain, Hornell, at his own expense, visited all the areas where coracles were or had been used and made, and recorded their history, present manufacture, and usage, through interviews, research and photographic record.

Everyone with an interest in coracles owes James Hornell a huge dept of gratitude.

Fortunately Hornell's pioneering work was carried forward by Dr Jenkins in his book *Nets and Coracles*, which was published in 1974. This was the result of many years of original research. It was extended by another book, *The Coracle*, originally published in 1988 and very recently revived.

Geraint Jenkins was for a number of years a member of the teaching staff of Reading University, probably the foremost university specialising in rural and agricultural affairs. He then went on to become the curator of the then Welsh Folk Museum (now the Museum of Welsh Life), and was regarded as a leading historian of the fishing industry and our maritime heritage. It is difficult to overestimate his contribution to the study of coracles.

WHAT IS A CORACLE?

Before it is possible to embark on the difficult task of sifting such historical data as there is, it is necessary to establish what constitutes a coracle. Until this is done, it is impossible to interpret references to 'coracles' and 'curraghs' – expressions used with indiscriminate frequency, but not consistent accuracy, in early literature.

An accurate description of a coracle is crucial to establish the approximate earliest date their existence became known. There is no authoritative definition of 'a coracle', but there are many descriptions, both oral and written, from which the essential elements of what *constitutes* a coracle can be ascertained.

Coracles – definition

Not surprisingly, different names are used in different countries for what is essentially the same type of craft.

The Concise Oxford Dictionary's definition of a coracle is 'a small boat of wickerwork covered with watertight material used on Welsh and Irish lakes and rivers'. This is a very unsatisfactory description, as it ignores the fact that coracles are – or were – to be found not only in Wales and Ireland, but also in England, Scotland and other parts of the world.

In England, in addition to the word 'coracle', the following names are to be found in the Wye area: 'thorrocle', 'truckle' and 'coble'. Another expression used is 'coricles'. The late Eustace Rogers (about whom much more later) pronounced coracles in this way when talking about the craft he used to make and use. In an 1861 publication entitled the *Book of South Wales, the Wye and the Coast*, the authors Mr and Mrs S. C. Hall suggest that the word 'trug' is a Saxon derivation of coracle.

In Scotland, coracles are commonly called 'curraghs', but it is interesting to note that when Hornell writes about them, he refers to coracles which were used on the river Spey as 'Scottish coracles'. He also uses the expressions 'curock' and 'courich'.

In Ireland the names 'curragh' (English) and 'currach' (Irish) are used. Again, when referring to a Boyne curragh, Hornell refers to it as a 'coracle-shaped curragh'.

When writing about coracles in Wales, Geraint Jenkins refers to the Welsh words 'cwrwgl', 'cwrwg', and 'corwg'. Moreover, Hornell uses the same words as Jenkins, and goes on to assert that the word 'coracle' is derived from the Welsh word 'cwrwgl', whereas the English word 'curragh' refers to a larger sea-going craft, and derives from the word 'corwc'. (In passing, it should be observed that, at a coracle regatta held at Cilgerran in West Wales in 1997, the commentator, when describing an English coracle entry, called it a 'canoe'.)

In India, says Hornell, the Tamil word 'parisil' is used when referring to a coracle and 'argili' in Telugi. In the east of Tibet, he says, the expression used is 'ku dru', and according to the *Lonely Planet Guide to Vietnam*, coracles there are called 'thung chai'.

When referring to Iraqi coracles Hornell uses the expressions 'guffa' and 'quffa'.

Finally, in North America the Native American coracle is called a 'bull boat'.

Coracle construction

James Hornell states that: ' ... the old design of a coracle as it exists today [i.e. in the 1930s] consists of a broad ovate, latticed framework in the form of a shallow, wide-mouthed basket, covered with calico waterproofed outside with a covering of pitch and tar.' This aptly describes a lot of coracles – but not all. For instance, the Teifi coracle, still commonly found today, is roughly 'kidney-shaped'.

Another description is to be found in a book entitled *Traditional British Crafts* (author unknown), page 290: 'A coracle is basically a waterproof basket, an open lattice covered with some impermeable material. It is light enough for one man to carry on his back, draws only two or three inches and is very manoeuvrable. It can be paddled one-handed.'

From these descriptions it is suggested that the following criteria emerge when considering what is a coracle:

1. It must be small enough to be manoeuvrable.
2. It must be light enough to be capable of being carried by one person.
3. It must be capable of being paddled with a single paddle.
4. Its frame should be constructed of narrow wooden laths or splints.
5. It should be covered with animal hide, canvas, calico or similar material, made waterproof with pitch and tar, bitumastic paint, or a similar waterproofing substance.

Applying these criteria, it can confidently be stated that coracles are, or were, to be found in England, India, Iraq, Ireland, North America, Scotland, Tibet, Vietnam, and Wales.

Since the late James Hornell wrote definitive books on coracles throughout the world based on information obtained between the two world wars, the only other substantial contribution to this subject is to be found in the writings of Dr J. Geraint Jenkins, principally in the 1970s. He wrote exclusively about English and Welsh coracles.

Many other people have written about coracles, of whom Professor Sean McGrail is an outstanding example. However, when they refer to 'coracles' they do so as a small part of a general subject. So far as the global view of coracles is concerned, there have been very considerable changes since Hornell carried out his studies.

Except in Vietnam, the traditional use of coracles is in decline.

In addition, there have been changes in the materials with which coracles are made. For instance, paint has been substituted for pitch and tar as the method of waterproofing coracles. But even more fundamental is the use of fibreglass in place of wooden laths, particularly in the Teifi and Tywi areas of west Wales.

Notes

[1] Professor T. Watkins, *Prehistoric Coracles in Fife* (IJNO 9, 1980), pp. 277-86.

[2] Professor S. McGrail, *Ancient Boats in North West Europe* (Longman, 1987), p. 186.

Chapter One
NATIVE AMERICAN BULL BOATS

Anyone beginning a serious study of coracles of the world should start with the Native American bull boat, because it was so well documented when it was being used to the full, and because it probably provides the best available evidence of what the first coracles were like and how they were used.

James Hornell, in his seminal work *Water Transport*, referred to the bull boat as 'a very crude and clumsily constructed type of skin boat'. That description, if somewhat unkind, is nonetheless accurate. Bull boats are, however, of considerable importance in a consideration of coracles and allied crafts generally. They were made and used by the Plains Indians. Amongst those who used them were the Assinboin, Cherokee, Kansa, Omaha, Mandan, Arikara, and Hidatsa. The greatest quantity of information available relates to the three last-mentioned tribes. Bull boats have not been used since the mid nineteenth century.

There is some evidence of 'coracle usage' in parts of the United States other than the upper Missouri . This will be dealt later, but for the meantime concentration will be upon bull boat usage in what is now North Dakota.

Importance of the Native American bull boat
Until the twentieth century, the bull boat was used regularly and extensively in the area inhabited by the Plains Indians in what is now North Dakota, USA. Moreover, there is good reason to believe that that usage occurred without substantial change for at least a thousand years. One of the most important uses of the bull boat was for the ferrying of firewood and meat, following the biannual bison hunt, back to a Plains village.

Permanent houses in the form of earth lodges in the Plains area began to appear about a thousand years ago. Before that, the tribes would have been wholly nomadic and thus would not have needed the waterborne transport necessary to service largely permanently occupied villages.[1]

It is suggested that a close study of the bull boat provides the best available opportunity of discovering what the earliest coracles would have been like. This is particularly important, as information about coracles over a similar period is sparse. The bull boat is by a long chalk the most primitive type of coracle, and accordingly a study of it is the best place to begin a consideration of coracles generally.

Sociologically, bull boat manufacture and use is of importance as it reveals a window on the respective roles of men and women of the Plains tribes. Women always made bull boats, and were the most frequent users of them. The only other example of women being so employed concerns the provision of an Iraqi quffa for the now defunct Exeter Maritime Museum, by H. G. Balfour-Paul CMG, who was then the British Ambassador in Iraq. It was made for him by a blind Iraqi woman: it is not known if this was exceptional.

All other 'coracles' known to me were, and are, invariably made by men – with the exception of their covering in the river Teifi area, which was always a female function.

Of all 'coracles', the bull boat is the best recorded. In the sixteenth, seventeenth and eighteenth centuries, considerable interest was taken in the American Indian by a limited number of Europeans and United States citizens. A number of them, as well as being accomplished writers, were competent artists, the best-known being George Catlin and Karl Bodmer. As a result, there is a wealth of reliable information about the Native American bull boat over a substantial period of time when what is now North Dakota was not part of the USA.

More than any other 'coracle', the bull boat played a considerable part in the life of a Plains village, as will become apparent when bull boat usage is specifically dealt with later. Unlike most other 'coracles', it was essentially a temporary craft. Its significance is that it provides sound evidence of the genesis of coracles; its variety and number of uses distinguishes the bull boat from other 'coracles'.

To make a bull boat, virtually no tools were required, and the process was much less arduous or sophisticated than the making of a dugout canoe – its only rival as the oldest craft known to man.

Of significance are the reasons for the disappearance of the bull boat. James Hornell attributes the passing of the buffalo herds as the reason why they were no longer made. I discussed this matter with members of the Hidatsa Tribe on the Fort Berthold Reservation in October 1999. They agreed, but said that other reasons were the fact that the type of willow needed for laths became unavailable, and the Native Americans were essentially pragmatic people who on becoming aware of more advanced forms of water transport ceased to use their own cruder and less efficient craft .

Lastly, the bull boat plays a significant part in the consideration of the 'Madog legend', which will be referred to specifically later.

Construction of bull boats and paddles

According to Hornell:
> ... the usual form was that of a circular bowl, flattened at the bottom and with vertical sides. The framework consisted of willow rods, spaced widely apart, half the number running at right angles to those of the other half, bound together with thongs at the crossings and with ends turned up abruptly at the bilges. Other withies were tied round the projecting ends to form a circular gunwale. Over this rude framing a cover, made of a couple of buffalo hides, was stretched with the edges reflected over the gunwale and lashed down ...

This description cannot be improved on, save to say that in all the bull boats I have seen, single hides were used.

Edwin Tappar Adney and Howard Chapelle[2] suggest that bull boats were built upwards on the skin. Whilst this is logical and would permit the boat to be tailored to the size of the skin, it was not the method used by the late Anna Crowsfoot (Mrs J. Y. Eagle), a Plains Indian, when she made a bull boat for the State Historical Society of the North Dakota Heritage Centre (Fig. 1:1). I examined two bull boats at the North Dakota Heritage Centre in September 1999, one having been made by Anna Crowsfoot in 1955, and the other many years earlier (Plate 1). I also had the good fortune to meet Anna Crowsfoot's grandson, Billie Joe Jacobs, who as a very small boy was present when she made the bull boat mentioned above. Billie Joe had a reasonably clear recollection of its being made, and particularly remembered her flensing the hide with a wood and metal scraper which was identical to an ancient flensing tool on display at the Heritage Centre. Another bull boat was on display in the Smithsonian Institution at Bronx, New York in 1990.

Furthermore, I was sent photographs of a third bull boat collected by Dr Gilbert Wilson in 1916 and now in the possession of the Science Museum of Minnesota. Dr Wilson also provided its dimensions. Additionally, I examined a replica bull boat in October 1999 at Knife River (Plate 2).

Another replica bull boat was built by the Newport coracle-maker, Terry Kenny, from photographs and descriptions provided by the North Dakota Heritage Centre. It is currently in the National Coracle Centre, Cenarth, west Wales (Plate 3).

Fig 1 : 1
Anna Crowsfoot (Mrs J. Y. Eagle)
making a bull boat.

Descriptions of these bull boats are:

Newer Dakota boat
Diameter 127 cm (50"); depth 38 cm (15"); 8 rib construction with 2 circular frames;
Covering: bison hide; lashings: leather thongs; date of construction, 1955 (Billie Joe Jacobs disputes this, saying it was in 1957).

Older Dakota Boat
Diameter 159 cm; (52.5"); depth 38.5 cm (15"); covering: cow hide; no of laths: 6 lengthwise, 5 transverse, 2 circular, lashings: cloth strips; used by Native Americans just before 1900.

Minnesota Boat
Dimensions from Science Museum – diameter 55"; depth 18"; Covering: cow's hide; ribs made of red willow; lashings: cloth and raw hide; there is some uncertainty as to its age, but it was probably collected by Dr.Wilson in 1916.

Rather surprisingly, the laths of the older Dakota boat appeared to have been cleaved or thinned to facilitate bending, which is a somewhat sophisticated process for such a primitive craft, although regularly encountered in British, Indian and Vietnamese Coracles .

Hides

The hair of the hide, wrote Gilbert Wilson, in his PhD thesis *Waheenee – an Indian Girl's Story* (1927), is always on the outside. The purpose of this is so that there be a defined fore and aft of a bull boat. Without this, the lay of the hair would not be known, and the craft's progress through the water reduced due to friction being caused if the boat were to move against the lay of the hair. The tail is not removed. It is used not only to indicate the craft's front and back, but also it can be used to join two or more bull boats together.

Paddles

The paddles were cut from a cottonwood log. There are two distinctive features in bull boat paddles. Firstly, they all have a large hole cut in the centre of the blade. It is shaped like two triangles on top of one another. The purpose of it is to prevent the paddle *'wobbling in the current'*. This feature is unique amongst coracles, but is found in the rudder of some Chinese junks, according to David Goddard, the former Director of the now defunct Exeter Maritime Museum.

Secondly, on the blade of the paddle stripes, pony hoofprint shapes and moccasin track shapes were printed, using warm buffalo fat and red ochre. They signified brave deeds by the bull boat maker's husband (Plate 4).

Portage and paddling technique

Thus G. Catlin, writing in 1846, describing bull boat paddling techniques, said:

> The woman in paddling these awkward tubs, stands in the bow, and makes the stroke with the paddle, by reaching it forward in the water and drawing it to her, by which means she pulls the canoe along with some considerable speed.[3]

A slightly different description is given by Gilbert Wilson, narrating a conversation he had with a member of the Hidatsa tribe at the beginning of the last century. '... a bull boat is usually paddled by one person, kneeling (or sometimes sitting) in the forward part of the boat and dipping the paddle before'. Waheenee also describes the paddler kneeling rather than standing. A similar technique is used by Indian 'coracle' paddlers and by the users of Boyne and Donegal currachs. It is submitted that Catlin's description of a paddler standing is probably in error. Waheenee also describes how when a bull boat is towing one or more other bull boats, then the woman paddler will be joined by her husband. The norm, however, is for the woman to paddle on her own.

Ice in the Missouri was a great source of concern to bull boat users when paddling their craft in winter.

Catlin describes another way in which bull boats were used:

> The old chief having learned that we were to cross the river, gave directions to one of the women, who took upon her head the skin canoe (more familiarly called in this country 'the bull boat') which she carried to the water's edge, and placing it in the water, made signs for us three to get in. When we were in and seated flat on its bottom, she stepped before the boat and pulling it along waded toward the deeper water, with her back toward us, carefully with the other hand attending to her dress, which seemed to be but a light slip and floating upon the surface, until the water was above her waist, when it was instantly turned off over her head and thrown ashore; and she boldly plunged forward, swimming and drawing the boat with one hand, which she did with apparent ease.

Wilson wrote that when not in the water bull boats were carried over the paddler's head, and sometimes on a dog travois when it was necessary to carry it a distance over land. This latter practice is similar to that of the Tibetans, who will use a coracle in the river and then dismantle it so that it can be transported over land.

Uses

The uses of bull boats were many and varied, and included the following:

1. The collection of firewood, a valuable commodity, and the transporting of it back to the village.

2. After the tribe had killed a substantial number of buffaloes, sometimes as many as forty, the animals would be skinned, the meat cut up and loaded into a number of bull boats, which had been made on the spot by the women, and then transported back to the village by water. To achieve this a number of bull boats would be lashed together, with the manned craft being on outside (Fig. 1:2).

3. When tribe members set out to steal horses, they would travel by bull boat, which they would leave behind once the horses had been secured.[4]

4. They would be similarly used for raiding enemies.

5. According to C. Gilman, bull boats were often propped up on their paddles to provide protection for the holes on top of the earth lodges through which smoke escaped.[5]

6. They were generally used for ferrying people across various rivers in the Plains area (Fig.1:3).

The Madog Legend
A great deal has been written about this subject, but consideration is confined to the relevance of the bull boat to the arguments advanced.

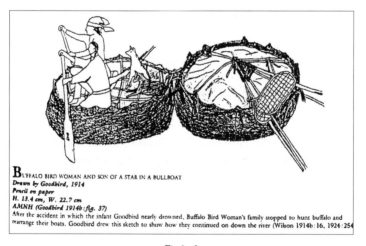

BUFFALO BIRD WOMAN AND SON OF A STAR IN A BULLBOAT
Drawn by Goodbird, 1914
Pencil on paper
H. 13.4 cm, W. 22.7 cm
AMNH (Goodbird 1914b:fig. 37)
After the accident in which the infant Goodbird nearly drowned, Buffalo Bird Woman's family stopped to hunt buffalo and rearrange their boats. Goodbird drew this sketch to show how they continued on down the river (Wilson 1914b:16, 1924:254

Fig 1 : 2
Sketch of two bull boats lashed together.
("Buffalo Bird Woman and Son of a Star": artist Goodbird, 1914).

Fig 1 : 3
Bull boat being used for ferrying passenger across the river, North Dakota.

It will be sufficient to have regard to three books for this purpose, namely Catlin's book (already referred to); *Madoc – The Making of a Myth* by Professor Gwyn A. Williams; and *The Forgotten People*, by Tony Williams.

One of the arguments for saying that the Mandan Indians were the descendants of Madog, the twelfth-century north Welsh Prince, and his followers, is the suggested similarity between bull boats and Welsh coracles. Professor Williams refers to '... bull boats – round skin and wickerwork craft *similar to Welsh Coracles*'.[6] Catlin asserts that 'Mandan canoes [by which he means bull boats] are *exactly* the Welsh coracle.'

Finally, Tony Williams, the most recent writer, and a Welshman who has seen contemporary west Walian coracles, strongly argues that the similarity between the bull boat and Welsh coracles is one of the strongest reasons in support of Mandans being descended from Madog and his supporters.[7]

Whatever the merits of other arguments for supporting the link, it is submitted that no credence can be put on coracle/bull boat joint identity for these reasons. Firstly, to talk about 'Welsh coracles' as a single group is not helpful. There is great deal of difference between, say, Teifi, Dee, Cleddau, and Dwyryd coracles. Moreover, it is submitted that there is not, or was not, a Welsh coracle which is, or was, round or even oval in shape. There are, however, at least two English coracles which could be so described, namely Bewdley and Ironbridge coracles, the first-named being covered with hide, unlike contemporary Welsh coracles. The Spey curragh is also circular in shape and hide-covered .

Coracle usage in other parts of the USA

There is evidence that bull boats were used by white men in the Plains area, and to explore the Great Salt Lake.[8] Probably the best example is to be found in *Sgt Pryor's Failed Ride*, by Marilyn Hudson – herself part Hidatsa, and Curator of the Three Tribes Museum at New Town on the Fort Berthold Reservation. In it she describes how a member of Lewis and Clark's famous exploratory team, Sgt Nathaniel Pryor, had his horse stolen, whereupon he made himself a bull boat and returned to the others by river.

Hornell also had information about similar craft to bull boats being used in the Red River of the North Maritime Provinces and Keele river.

When exhibiting at the Northumberland Royal Show in the 1980s, Gerwyn Lewis, then the Director of the Greenwood Trust, and one who revived interest in coracles in the Ironbridge area, was spoken to by a seventy-year-old American who had been brought up on an Indian Reservation in Montana. The latter said that he remembered seeing 'coracles' in use on his reservation. They were made with withy laths, and had a paper cover which was impregnated with shellac.

'The bull boat or something like it, was also made by Indians of the south eastern United States', according to an article which appeared in *The Florida Anthropologist.*[9] The writer, William T. Neill, examined a number of reliable sources. He produced evidence of usage in the area of what is today Augusta, Georgia, and postulated that the first record of such usage was in 1737. Interestingly, he described that such craft were of the folding variety. There is no evidence of folding bull boats in the Plains area of North Dakota. He concludes that:

> ... evidently skin boats were used by the Chicksaw, Mikasuki and

Muskogee, at least, as well as by white traders and explorers. The area of known use included southern Georgia, and immediately adjacent areas of South Carolina, northern Florida, and perhaps eastern Alabama (the Okchai country).

When considering this usage it must be remembered that the local settlers of Georgia and South Carolina were largely from the British Isles, and they had friendly relations with the Indians. One could not disagree with the proposition of Neill when he says: 'It is at least conceivable that the early British settlers introduced the coracle to the South eastern Indians...' In support of his proposition he cites the fact that '... among the Missouri river tribes, the bull boat was greatly favoured, for wooden dugouts or rafts were not easily manufactured in the Plains region where trees were scarce. In the South East, however, trees were abundant, and the dugout was almost universally employed by the Indian tribes ...'

Modern United States 'coracle' usage
The Coracle Society of England and Wales has a number of American members, and by far and away the largest number of enquiries to the Society's website comes from the United States. These, however, are concerned entirely with British and Irish coracles. There is evidence of British and Irish-style coracles being made in the United States by people such as George O'Bryan of Stony Bottom, West Virginia, and Stanley Joseph of Penobscot Bay, Maine. Sadly, however, there is no sign of a rival of interest in Native American bull boats by those who today live in the United States.

Notes
[1] Stanley A. Ahler et al, *People of the Willows* (1991), p. 27.
[2] Edwin Tappar Adney and Howard Chapelle, *The Bark Canoe and Skin Boats of North America* (Washington, 1983), p. 220.
[3] G. Catlin, *Letters and Notes on the Manners, Customs and Conditions of the North American Indians*, Vol. 2 (Dover Publications, 1846), p. 138
[4] C. Gilman, *Way to Independence* (date unknown)
[5] 'Green Mounds for Redskins' in *Christian Science Monitor* (1939)
[6] Gwyn A. Williams, *Madoc: the making of a myth* (1979), p. 10
[7] T. Williams, *The Forgotten People* (Gomer, 1997), p. 147
[8] Roberts and Shackleton, *The Canoe* (Macmillan, 1983), p. 151
[9] W. T. Neil *The Florida Anthropologist*, Vol. 7 (1954), p. 11

Chapter Two
ENGLISH CORACLES

James Hornell claims that the British Coracle is 'derived from the same source as the bitumen-coated Quffa of Iraq and the skin covered coracles of India and Tibet'. It is assumed that he did not intend this list to be comprehensive, and his reasoning could apply equally to the Vietnamese coracle and the Native American bull boat. He rightly excludes the Irish curragh as a species from this group, because in form it is more akin to ancient plank-built boats, and is therefore more likely to have had similar origins. In view of its shape and riverine usage, the Boyne curragh is in essence a coracle, despite being called a curragh: its name being dictated linguistically in a country in which many and varied curraghs exist.

The nearest British coracle, in shape and, possibly, function, to the bull boat is the Ironbridge (Severn) coracle of England; as a result, English coracles as a group are now to be considered.

Sadly, there are very few references to English coracles in historical sources. The first can be found in *Britannia* by Camden (1586) when he wrote about the river Severn. He described the construction, handling and portage of a 'coracle' in terms instantly recognisable by anyone interested in contemporary coracles. He did not, however, mention where precisely he observed it.

Captain Richards, writing in his *Diary of the Marches of the Royal Army during the Great Civil War* (according to Hornell), gives a similar description. locating his sighting at Madeley, near Ironbridge.

A 1613 English pamphlet, dealing with an alleged witch, Mary Sutton, undergoing trial by drowning, shows a man in a coracle. This appears in an undated publication entitled *Witches and Witchcraft*.

It is claimed that 'King Edward II's French expeditionary force was equipped with Severn coracles for catching fish in Lent'[1]

A booklet entitled *Craft Tools of Yesterday* (1979) states that the Sussex 'trug' is thought to have originated with the work of Thomas Smith, a native of Hurstmonceaux in Sussex, who is said to have based his design on that of the coracle, and who first exhibited his creation at the Great Exhibition of 1851.

There are numerous references to coracles having been used by the followers of Boudicca and Hereward the Wake, but there is an absence of hard evidence for this, and it must therefore be relegated to supposition.

Most people with a casual knowledge of coracles tend to associate them exclusively with Wales and Ireland, but in their heyday of 1914 there were more coracles in use on the Severn than any other river in the British Isles. Indeed, according to Hornell such usage stretched from Welshpool to Bewdley, a distance of some sixty miles, and Jenkins said that even up to 1939 they were in use for over thirty miles between Shrewsbury and Arley.[2] 'So considerable was the demand for coracles in the Ironbridge district at the beginning of the 20th century that a school was established where the principles of coracle manipulation were taught.'

Because of its industrial history and, particularly, its famous bridge, the Severn at Ironbridge attracted the attention of a number of well-known painters in whose paintings and drawings a coracle often appeared. 'A View on the River Severn' and 'The Cast Iron Bridge near Coalbrookdale' by William Williams (c. 1740/1798), and 'View of the Cast Iron Bridge' after Michael Angelo Rooker (1743-1801), are but a few examples. They are referred to in *A View from the Ironbridge*.[3]

Whilst, undoubtedly, the English Severn had more coracles on it than any other river in the United Kingdom, coracles also were, and are, to be found on the Wye, Avon and Teme. Moreover, there is some evidence that coracles were used on the Thames. Coracles on the Severn were not confined to Ironbridge. They were also to be found in Shrewsbury, Bridgnorth, Bewdley and possibly Tewkesbury. Coracles found in these areas will be dealt with later; for the moment concentration will be on the Ironbridge coracle.

Many coracles are being made today in England, as far afield as Norfolk and Cornwall, due largely to the pioneering revival coracle-making courses started by the Greenwood Trust of Ironbridge, and Bewdley Museum's then curator, Charles Fogg, a Bridgnorth man. It should be noted, however, that this new wave of coracles is being made purely for recreational purposes and not, as in former times, as working craft.

IRONBRIDGE CORACLES

Hornell was the first person to call the type of coracle made and used on the Severn in the Coalbrookdale area an 'Ironbridge Coracle'. This nomenclature has been in regular use for very many years. Such a description is helpful because there are a number of other 'bowl-shaped coracles' – found in India, Tibet and Vietnam, and elsewhere.

There are a number of reasons why this type of coracle is the best-known of all English coracles. Firstly, the unique position of Ironbridge in industrial history has ensured that more than average notice of all facets of life in the area has been taken. Furthermore, the writings of Hornell, Jenkins and, particularly, Brian Waters in *Severn Tide* (1947) and *Severn Stream* (1949) make it clear that an unusually large number of coracles were to be found in this part of Shropshire. This was no doubt due to the varied use made of the coracle in the Ironbridge area.

Probably the best-known family of coracle-makers and users anywhere in the British Isles is the Rogers family of Ironbridge. The last of the line, Eustace Rogers, lived and practised his craft within the shadow of the famous Ironbridge until he died in 2004.

The Greenwood Trust of Coalbrookdale, in addition to setting up the coracle-making courses already referred to, was also responsible for reviving the annual coracle regatta on the Severn, which had come to an end in the 1930s.

The Ironbridge Gorge Museum Trust, an institution whose influence in industrial, social and engineering history is worldwide, has taken a particular interest in – and has done much to publicize – the local coracle, and the Rogers family.

Ironbridge Coracle Usage
These were many and varied. Principal among them were the following:

- Transportation of people and property (some lawful, some not)
- Net fishing
- Laying of eel lines
- Rabbit rescuing and capture
- Securing driftwood

- Rescuing people and animals
- Recovering cadavers
- Poaching

Transportation

In days gone by a number of local people had to cross the Severn to get to work in Coalbrookdale. Bridges were few and far between and it wasn't until the beginning of the twentieth century that a bridge was available to them for which they did not have to pay a toll. They objected strongly to paying these tolls and realised that they could circumvent such payment by acquiring and using a coracle. According to James Hornell, before the building of the free bridge, when the people of Jackfield and Coalport acquired the means of crossing the river without paying, '... [nearly] every cottager had his own coracle, hung in a tree when not in use ...' In *Coracles, Miners and Other Memories,*[4] A J Mugridge wrote about coracle usage on the Severn in the Ironbridge area at about the turn of the twentieth century. He described how coracles were made on the Werps (an area of Ironbridge) by Frank Poole and Arthur Williams, who would often take people across the Severn in coracles. He went on to say that 'most of the folks down that end of Jackfield had coracles'.

Coracles also played a very considerable part in the unlawful conveyance of poachers – but this will be dealt with later!

Net Fishing

Geraint Jenkins wrote that 'A River Board bye-law of 1890 severely restricted, and the Salmon and Freshwater Fisheries Act of 1923 spelt the doom of, coracle netting on the Severn.' Eustace Rogers was unique in that he was the only person living who had personal recollection of lawful net fishing on the Severn at Ironbridge. I had the good fortune of knowing Eustace since the time that he made two coracles for me in the 1980s. During this period he told me about net fishing. Eustace explained that whereas now there are not any salmon to be found in the Severn at Ironbridge, this had not been the case in years gone by. Indeed, he had in his famous shed a book which recorded the number of salmon taken in the nineteenth century.

Eustace Rogers has been interviewed at considerable length on two occasions in the past, and transcripts of these recordings were made. The first was by a member of the Ironbridge Gorge Museum staff in 1982, and the other by members of the Greenwood Trust in 1991.

In the Greenwood Trust interview (1991), Eustace gave a full description of how net fishing was carried out. From this description, it is apparent that the Ironbridge method of net fishing was very different from that practised on the rivers Teifi, Towy and Taf of west Wales. In Ironbridge, only one man was present in a coracle. One end of the net was secured to the bank by pegs. When this was done, the single coracleman would paddle with one hand to the centre of the river with the remainder of the net. He never paddled to beyond the centre of the river. He explained that although licensed to fish with a net, the fisherman could not go beyond halfway, as the Severn was a 'free' river and no one was allowed to put a barrier across it. When the coracleman had reached the centre, he returned to the bank from which he had embarked. By doing this he had cordoned off a section of the river. He then beat the water with a beating pole, which was 'like a broom stick with a big leather disc on it.' The net was described by Rogers as follows: 'It's three nets. There's the outwalling, which is a big mesh. The outwalling on each side, but the net that's catching him is the middle of those two. He takes that through the big mesh, that's a small mesh. He takes it through, he's like a rabbit in a purse net. Canna get out of it ...'

Eustace Rogers had two of these nets in his shed. He said there were not many who fished in this way in his day (he was born in 1914), and he hadn't heard his father talking of many either. Plate 5 shows William Rogers, who is one of Eustace's earliest relatives. It is clear that he is in an Ironbridge coracle and has a net with him.

The Severn coraclemen would walk as much as ten miles upstream carrying their coracles and nets. They would sometimes go as far as the outskirts of Shrewsbury. During my conversations with him, Eustace Rogers said that net fishing virtually stopped overnight and, somewhat to his surprise, no-one attempted to fish unlawfully with nets thereafter.

The laying of eel (or 'night') lines
When discussing net fishing, Eustace Rogers also mentioned the

practice of laying eel lines or as they were known in Shrewsbury, 'night' lines. He said that this practice came to an end not long after the demise of net fishing.

In the Greenwood Trust interview (1991), Eustace gives a full account of laying eel lines and the part the coracle played in it. At page 1 he states: '... me Dad or me Uncle would take me with them when they went line-laying for eels ... they would take their lines and their bait with them. Their bait would be stone roach, which is commonly known as jack sharps and bullnobs ... my job was to get some big dock leaves (which were used for lining the nets into which the catch would ultimately be put) ... their line would reach across the river about three times. It was set across the river, not down the river. It was set across the river about three times. There was links, ten links fastened onto this line, and a link about three foot six to four foot long with a hook on the end of it ...' He then went on to describe how the lines were baited and how the baited hooks would be placed on a dock leaf in a basket.

He continued:

> Now you couldn't interfere with that line because they never touched the bank. They'd got some stones in the coracle about like your fist, and they would fasten the end of the line around the stone. He'd drop that in perhaps ten feet of water. Now he'd paddle directly across the river, straight across, and every so often he would put a link on, only tie it in a bow because the more anything pulled the tighter it was getting, but it was so easy to undo next morning ... and before he'd got to the other side, then he'd turn back again ... with going across the river like that, the flow of water was holding the link away. The next morning it wasn't all tangled up when they came to pull it up when there was an eel on it ...They'd lay several miles. Then when they'd finished, they'd carry the coracles to where they started and have the night on the bank. As soon as it was daylight, they'd got things made a purpose as they could find that line and that's why they could tell you the depth of the river and what kind of bottom anywhere, for miles up and miles down. Then he'd be sitting with his legs apart in the coracle pulling the line over the front and as he come to eel, he'd get a piece of rag and he'd snatch that eel off and put it in the back behind him, because there was a board under the seat to stop them coming through to his feet. He'd undo the link, he'd put that down and this [is] how he would go on. That is my early recollections ...

In the Ironbridge Gorge museum interviews (1982), Eustace Rogers described how on occasions when they were fishing with nets, if the weather was frosty they would 'go after moorhens'. To achieve this, they would use the same link that they used for eel catching '... [it was] about a yard long, and bait as the same as for an eel.' Rogers explained that moorhen was a local delicacy.

Rabbit rescuing and capture
Hornell writes as follows: '... rabbits, too, driven from their burrows by the flood, scurry to higher ground. Here they often find themselves marooned on islets surrounded by swirling waters. Others seek precarious refuge in the tops of partially submerged hedgerows. Now out come the coraclemen ... to net the rabbits huddled in fright on their island refuges.'

This is undoubtedly a true account of what happened when the Severn burst its banks; a not infrequent occurrence on this notoriously high-rising river. But it is not the full picture. In the time of Tommy Rogers (Eustace Rogers grandfather), and in Harry Rogers' (Eustace's father) younger days, they and others regularly poached rabbits over a large area of Shropshire. To do this, they used nets into which they drove the rabbits. On occasions they caught partridge by similar methods, and also took moles so that they could sell their skins. (Later in his life Harry Rogers took rabbits with the permission of landowners).

The unlawful operation always took place at night. Speed and silence of operation were vital. The nets used on these occasions were about fifty yards in length, so that they could be erected and dismantled swiftly. (The legitimate nets were approximately four times as long.) The rabbits were driven into the nets and killed almost immediately on arrival. Coracles were used for taking the nets across the river and for bringing the night's haul back. This enabled the poachers to return home without anything on them, to the frustration of the awaiting police. Often the coracles would be secreted at suitable points in advance. This brief description is based on the Greenwood Trust interview (1991) and Ironbridge Gorge Museum interviews (1982) of Eustace Rogers. Commenting on this type of poaching, Eustace, in the Greenwood Trust interview, said, '... I can bring you people now that when I meet them, they've said many times, 'We were reared on rabbits and fish off the poachers.' By God they were difficult times … they couldn't have done it without the coracle, even with the rabbit catching.'

Securing driftwood

During floods, felled timber becomes flotsam. Coraclemen up to the present time have rescued this timber, which could be a source of considerable danger if allowed to drift. When I visited Eustace Rogers in his shed in the 1980s he showed me a Shrewsbury coracle which had floated to Ironbridge when the Severn was unusually high, and which he had rescued. This apparently occurred shortly after the war.

A graphic account of the skills of the Ironbridge coracleman are provided in *Severn Valley Stories*, by Wilford Byford-Jones (1967), at p. 90 et seq.[5] One day he was watching Harry Rogers handling his coracle on the Severn near Ironbridge. He became aware of the branch of a big tree which was moving very quickly under the great iron bridge. Byford-Jones describes what happened thereafter as follows:

> Obviously the old man was intent on waylaying it, but how he could do so in so frail a craft I could not imagine. I watched him take up position in a line with the object and feared that he would be swept aside. As the long object approached Rogers turned the coracle to the right, then moved alongside it with remarkable speed. Next moment I saw him knock a nail, to which a rope was attached, into the floating object. It was, I now saw, the limb of a big tree, felled on the steep bank of the Severn in Wales during a storm. It had come surging downstream to England. He allowed a length of rope to run out of his coracle, much as a fisherman would do with his line if he had caught a big salmon. Then, deftly, he tightened the rope and began to paddle to the side. To my amazement the surging progress was arrested. After some resistance it began to come to the side of the river in response to Roger's guidance. No-one but Harry Rogers could have done that: to see it was as exciting as seeing a cow boy at a rodeo. As I watched him drag the monster trunk out of the water to take its place in his 'cemetery of flotsam', the angler joined me. When I joined Rogers in his 'cemetery', I noticed, alongside the fallen limbs of trees, all of them former giants of the forest, several old wheelbarrows, an old fruit cart and two massive oak beams …

A record of a BBC interview with Harry Rogers was printed in an issue of *Country Magazine* in the 1940s. In it, he described how all the wood in his house was caught by him in his coracle when it came down the Severn. He said, 'It's all pitch pine, lovely it is ... when we caught the wood we dried it and seasoned it, and then we built the house ourselves.' The house he was referring to was on the banks of the Severn very close to the Iron Bridge, where his son Eustace lived until his death.

Rescuing people and animals

Wilford Byford-Jones continues describing his meeting with Harry Rogers after the flotsam incident. 'He [Rogers] had often visited a dozen marooned cottages in his coracle, delivering the post, food and, sometimes, coal. When the flood had continued to rise until it was dangerous for people to remain in cottages on low ground, he had led parties to the rescue. Only a coracle, propelled by its long rectangle blade of seasoned ash, could have made the journey in the tricky currents the flood caused.'

In his conversations with me, Eustace Rogers described occasions when he had rescued sheep and dogs from the river; a familiar experience for coraclemen on the west Wales rivers.

To prove that rescuing on the Severn was not the sole province of the Rogers family, resort must be had to an account of a remarkable rescue of a little girl by one Jacky Harrison as described by Waters:

> The fall in the Severn between Jackfield and Coalport is very rapid, and the stream is swifter here than anywhere along the English Severn. The most brilliant feat of watermanship ever accomplished with a coracle within living memory was performed along this reach of river, some twenty-five years ago. A little girl had fallen into the Severn with the stream in full flood; Jacky Harrison, who used a coracle to go to work at the Coalport China works, went to her rescue. The child was floating downstream, borne up by the wind that had gathered under her thick plaid skirt; indeed, she would probably have sunk but for the speed of the river. About the most difficult thing to do in a coracle is to travel on a current in flood and keep your vessel under control. Jacky Harrison, however, worked his coracle with such skill that he drew level with the moving child, but even in this position he was unable to rescue her without

upsetting his coracle. Instead he edged the floating child out of the main stream, bringing her gradually nearer to the opposite bank, until, after almost a mile he brought her safely ashore at Coalport ... [6]

Recovering cadavers

In the era of Tommy and Harry Rogers, before the emergency services were not as well organised and available as they are today, there was a need for someone to carry out the unpleasant task of recovering dead bodies from the river Severn. This fell to the Rogers family and their coracles. In tape C20 of the Ironbridge Gorge Museum interviews, Eustace Rogers dealt with this gruesome subject, and his grandfather's part in it, saying '... he'd saved eight lives and he'd retrieved thirty bodies out. And me Dad and me Uncle Jim, they assisted him in many of these and they carried it on after. I can remember them sitting down one day and counting and it was over eighty that they had retrieved. And never had a halfpenny. Always refused.'

He then went on to recount an instance when his grandfather retrieved the body of a boy drowned whilst swimming in the Severn. A collection was held for his grandfather and half a sovereign was raised. It was offered to Tommy Rogers, who said, 'Now you take it to that lad's parents ... they need it more than I do.'

Mention has already been made that the coraclemen had acquired total knowledge of the river Severn's bed as a result of their net fishing and eel line laying. It was apparent talking to Eustace Rogers that he had acquired this knowledge from his grandfather, father and uncle. Moreover, he was frequently consulted by the police when someone had drowned, as he was able to predict where the body would surface. He said that he had recovered about ten bodies personally and had never accepted or expected any remuneration for doing so.

Poaching

In the heyday of the Ironbridge coracle there were many men who made a full-time living by poaching – so much so, that there were more policemen in Ironbridge than any other town in the area. Without the use of a coracle such men would not have been able to follow their occupation. A number of the old Severn bargemen carried coracles on their barges. As they were often the sole suppliers of information to the isolated villages, they would spread disturbing rumours which ensured that local people would remain indoors at night, thus facilitating the bargemen's poaching activities. This information is derived from general conversations I had with Eustace Rogers, and Eustace's interviews with the Ironbridge Gorge Museum staff (1982).

Another source of information on this subject is to be found in *Severn Stream*, where Waters writes as follows:

> ... many of the old-time coraclemen in Ironbridge were social survivals from life in prehistoric Britain. They lived in a country district without agricultural traditions, and were unable to adapt themselves to a life of industry. Some were suckers from the stock of the landed gentry, in whom pride of blood prevented their falling into step with the rank into which they were born. They became parasites on the feudal system, where the landlord preserved game, and expected his tenants to do likewise in the interests of his sport.
>
> At the beginning of the twentieth century, no fewer than a dozen Ironbridge families were supported by poaching. The mobility and weight-carrying capacity of the coracle made this possible, as well as the poachers' extra-territorial immunity from the police while afloat. The poachers, like most Severn men were known by quaint and individualistic nicknames ... So roomy and so great is the weight-carrying capacity of a coracle that enough rabbits and game to deck the inside of a poulterer's shop could be carried in one of these vessels. The speed and manoeuvrability of a coracle made escape and evasion easy to an active man, even when past his prime, and with a coracle a poacher was up to any trick. Sometimes when capture seemed almost certain the poacher would upset his coracle and swim for it, allowing his coracle to float down-stream ... At other times a coracle filled with game would be sunk in the river with stones, and retrieved at a more favourable opportunity ...

Although Waters' book was published in 1949, there is no doubt that the period he was writing about covered that of Eustace Roger's life. In the interviews mentioned earlier and in my conversations with him, Eustace corroborated all that Waters wrote. During the Ironbridge Gorge interviews, Eustace was asked if he considered the coracle had a significant role in poaching in the Ironbridge area. He replied, 'Yes, there is no doubt ... it was only due to the river they [the poachers] were able to lead the life they did'.

Modern coracling practices in Ironbridge

The emphasis so far has been on the way coracles have been used in the past, but there is a considerable interest in coracles in Ironbridge today. There are two main reasons for this: mention has already been made of the revival of the Ironbridge Gorge coracle regatta, which owes a great deal to the activities of the Greenwood Trust, and of its courses, which have been responsible for the making of large numbers of Ironbridge coracles, a great number of which are in evidence at the regatta (Plate 6).

The other reason is the very positive encouragement given by Eustace Rogers to would-be coracle-makers, his influence extending to the New World.

Personalities

Byford-Jones states that the Rogers family have been making coracles in the Ironbridge area for 360 years. The earliest member of that family who has been written about, William Rogers, has already been referred to. According to Eustace Rogers he was a purser on the barges.

The next in line was the most colourful of all the family, Tommy, born in 1843 (Fig. 2:1). He was a larger-than-life character in every sense. He was a huge man for his time, weighing over 18 stone. He had a prodigious capacity for alcohol. He ran the only school for teaching coracle-handling. He brought the last barge up the Severn, and was the last man to take a barge downstream to Gloucester and upstream to Shrewsbury. He was a lifelong poacher of considerable skill, who had many encounters with the police, bailiffs and landowners – most of which he won. He also was a swimming companion of Captain Matthew Webb, the first man to swim the channel. At the age of 79 he took part in a diving competition at Ironbridge regatta. Tommy Rogers died in 1924. Had he lived in the era of radio and television, doubtless even more would have been heard about him – as was the case with his son, Harry.

Harry Rogers (Fig. 2:2) was born in 1887. A great deal has been written about Harry. He started his life as a poacher with his father, Tommy, spending a lot of his time poaching rabbits, but he turned

Fig 2 : 1
Tommy Rogers, the most famous Ironbridge coracleman. He was father of Harry, and grandfather of Eustace.
Photo taken circa 1920.

legitimate in Eustace's early youth and became universally known as a rabbit catcher of exceptional skill. Typical examples of his skill as a coracle-handler and the ways in which he used his coracle to assist others in the neighbourhood have been already given. He made many coracles during his lifetime. He died in 1967. He was without doubt the finest coracleman on the Severn in his lifetime. He had an elder brother, James, who also was a skilled coracle-handler and lifesaver. Like Harry he took part in his father's poaching activities when young, but ceased following this way of life when he became older.

The last of the line was the octogenarian, Eustace Rogers, who has been written about even more than his father. His skills as a coracle-maker have always been in great demand, and in his time he made coracles for a wide variety of people and institutions. Some of the best-known purchasers of Eustace's coracles are General Hackett; Lord Boyd, the Trade Union leader; and Sir Peter Gadsden, a distinguished Lord Mayor of London. It mattered not to him who the purchaser was; everyone was treated with the same kindness and courtesy. He had a phenomenal memory, and his shed on the banks of the Severn close to the Iron Bridge was a place of infinite interest, full as it was with everything to do with poaching, coracles and agricultural life. He was born in 1914 and died in 2004, a bachelor. Sadly there is no-one of the Rogers family left to carry on the Ironbridge coracling tradition. Whilst the Rogers family's skill as makers and users of coracles is renowned, what is not so well-known is their skills as net-makers. In the Ironbridge Museum interview, Eustace Rogers said, '... they were really clever at net-making and I had been led to believe me Grandmother, Granny Rogers, was the best knitter of them all ... her nets are still in the shed. The family had been exceptionally good at net making; never bought any nets ... I have known gamekeepers ... send their nets to the old man to mend. It's much harder to mend a net than to make one ...'

Whilst there are not any members of the Rogers family to carry on the tradition, it has been maintained principally by two men, Gerwyn Lewis, a former Director of the Greenwood Trust at Coalbrookdale, and Terry Kenny, the present Chairman

Fig 2 : 2
Harry Rogers in around 1930-35, with passengers Susan and Alison Jones.

of the Coracle Society, the Newport coracle-maker who is now the instructor in charge of the highly successful coracle-making courses at Ironbridge (Plate 7). Nowadays, Ironbridge coracles are used almost entirely for leisure purposes, unlike in the time of Tommy and Harry Rogers when they were working craft. A throwback to the past is found in the experience of Terry Kenny, as related in 'From the river bank' in the May 1991 edition of the Coracle Society's newsletter. He wrote: 'I'd just closed the curtains on a frosty afternoon when there was a ring at the bell. Two large RSPCA men stood at the door. 'Are you the man who makes coracles?' I pleaded guilty. 'Perhaps you can help us. We've got a swan frozen in the middle of a pond and we need a flat-bottomed boat to slide across the ice to get to him. A chap at Market Drayton said to try you.' My Shrewsburyish coracle was in the back garden, and a few minutes later it was in the back of their Escort van speeding to the rescue. After a while they returned highly delighted with the result; the boat was perfect for the job and the swan was safe and sound.'

The Ironbridge coracle itself

Now to be considered are the shape, dimensions and materials used in the construction of Ironbridge Coracles past and present.

There is in the Museum of Welsh Life in Cardiff an Ironbridge coracle made by the late Harry Rogers and acquired by them from the City of Salford Museum in 1979 (Fig. 2:3). Its dimensions, as supplied by the Museum, are as follows:

Length 149.5 cm; width: (maximum) 110 cm; depth: 40 cm; length of paddle: 136 cm, and width of paddle blade: 17.3 cm.

The frame of the coracle and the paddle are painted green. The laths are of sawn ash, and the cover is canvas, impregnated with pitch and tar.

Eustace Rogers made an Ironbridge coracle for me in the 1980s (Plate 8). It is now part of the collection of coracles and allied craft housed in the National Coracle Centre, Cenarth, west Wales. Its dimensions are as follows: length: 1m 52 cm; width: 1m 22 cm; depth: 37 cm.

Although a paddle is not shown in the photograph of the Harry Rogers coracle it is identical in appearance to that shown in the photograph of the Eustace Rogers coracle.

Eustace Rogers told me that the dimensions of coracles varied according to the size of the person who would be using the coracle. The basic circular shape of the craft was constant, but its diameter and depth varied according to the height and, particularly, the weight of the person for whom it was made. Eustace also told me that with the closing of the local gas works it had become much more difficult to cover a coracle's skin with pitch and tar, the latter being difficult to come by. As a result, in recent times he had used bitumastic paint. It was also his practice to cover the frame with two thicknesses of calico or canvas.

Recently trials were carried out into various paddle shapes in the Ironbridge area. One of these was used to considerable effect by Simon Harper (then of Dawley), when he won a race at the Leintwardine regatta.

Coracles of a similar style were used in adjoining areas such as Bridgnorth and Quatt (Plate 9). This was probably made by Harry Rogers, and used on the pools at Dudmaston Hall in the 1930s. Referring to Bridgnorth, Hornell states that: 'only one coracle

Fig 2 : 3
An Ironbridge coracle made by Harry Rogers for the Museum of Welsh Life.

fisherman, Dick Brown, continues to use this type of craft. It is of typical Ironbridge form, and the paddle has ... [a] ... spade-shaped blade'. Hornell, no doubt, was writing about the pre-war period. Certainly there is no coracle tradition in the Bridgnorth area now, and hasn't been for some considerable time, although one coracle has been preserved and is kept in the Bridgnorth museum. Coracles of a different type were also to be found on other parts of the English Severn. The location of these coracles is certainly at Shrewsbury and Bewdley and possibly at Tewkesbury.

SHREWSBURY CORACLES

Introduction
The town with the second-strongest coracling tradition on the English Severn is Shrewsbury. This heritage is as a result of the activities of a coracleman who became well-known through rescuing footballs from the Severn behind Shrewsbury Town Football Club's goal.

History
Hornell quotes from *Salopian Shreds and Patches* thus: 'When George the third visited Worcester about the end of the last century [i.e. the eighteenth century], an old fisherman named Pedlow, living in Shrewsbury, felt a great wish to see his Majesty. Accordingly he made a voyage down the Severn in his coracle, being at the time more than eighty years old. The king graciously received the venerable Salopian, who returned to his native place, full of joy, and lived to the age of 97.' The Davies family of Shrewsbury (about whom more later) also made a river journey in a coracle, when they travelled from Shrewsbury to the tidal section of the Severn by coracle for charity in the 1980s.

Reference is made by Brian Waters to the activities of Jack Mytton, 'the mad squire of Halston', who, when his possessions were auctioned some one and a half centuries ago, owned two coracles as well as numerous poaching nets; these coracles almost certainly would have been Shrewsbury coracles as he lived his notorious life in the Shrewsbury area.

The same author paints a fascinating picture of the Severn in and around Shrewsbury in the mid twentieth century. He writes as follows:

> At Montford Bridge you may still meet a man looking like a turtle, as his coracle covers his back, for he is an amphibian about to take to the water. He is becoming a rarity, since, with one or two youthful exceptions, he is one of a diminishing band of ageing men. He will probably be alone, but in the earlier years of the century he was one of a school, who would leave Shrewsbury on a Saturday afternoon and not be home till dusk on Sunday. If you sighted the flotilla on its return to Coton Hill and Frankwell, you might notice that most of the coracles were drawing slightly more water than when they

embarked at Montford, and that this was not due to leaking vessels, but to the wild bounties along the Severn and its banks [presumably these 'bounties' were fish].

The river flows away from the bridge, and is joined by the winding Perry before encircling the Isle, where the Severn twists for five and a half miles around a low hill, before returning to within less than three hundred yards of its upper course. Many a coracle has been lifted out of the river and carried across the intervening yards. Before the industrial revolution a woollen mill stood on the bank of the lower bend, which received its power through a sluice from the upper course of the river. It is difficult to imagine industrialism in such a place, for except for the Queen Anne manor-house, two farms and a few cottages, there are no buildings on the Isle.

The squire, clear of eye, firm of speech, and active of limb at ninety-one, has the look of a man approaching seventy. A long time ago he rowed for three successive years in the Cambridge boat, and is probably the only rowing blue to use a coracle. Before the days of motor cars he and his wife would cross the Severn in their coracle when calling upon their neighbours. When dressed for an Edwardian garden-party they must often have passed a Salopian poacher in a similar 'acquatic conveyance' bound for a very different rendezvous.

My wife Mary and I have had the good fortune to join three generations of the Davies family (Fig. 2:4) on the Severn at this location in coracles. Their coracles were put in the water at one side of a field belonging to the Holloway's farm at the Isle, Bicton near Shrewsbury. They then travelled for some five and a half miles and arrived back at the other side of this same field. I made this journey several times; my wife once. During these journeys, we learned an immense amount about life on the Severn near Shrewsbury, principally from the late Jack Davies. It is doubtful if much of this information would have been forthcoming if enquiries had been made in a more formal way on land!

The Isle was then owned by the late Humphrey Sandford, a descendant of 'the Squire' mentioned earlier by Waters. He and his late wife Sheila took a keen interest in coracles. Through John Davies (Jack's son), I learnt of a coracle possessed by the Sandfords which was quite unlike any other coracle he had come across. Moreover there is not a reference to it in any of the works of Hornell or Jenkins.

I learnt from the late Sheila Sandford and her late father Duncan Robertson of Llangollen that it had belonged to a relative of Mrs Sandford's and hailed from the river Dwyryd in North Wales. (This craft will be described fully in a later chapter.) John Davies made an excellent replica of it which is now in the National Coracle Centre, Cenarth, west Wales.

Incidentally, I recall Jack Davies describing a similar incident to that described earlier by Waters, when he and his associates waved to the local squire as they travelled past him in their coracles. Indeed it might well have been the 'squire' mentioned by Waters, but the date of the incident is not certain.

Fig. 2:5 shows a typical Shrewsbury coracleman at the end of the nineteenth century, and Fig. 2:6 shows a coracle in use in Shrewsbury during the floods of *c*.1936.

This short passage on the history of the Shropshire coracle would not be complete without further reference to the Davies family. They are to Shrewsbury as the Rogers family are to Ironbridge.

The Davieses have been making and using coracles for some six generations. James Davies lived from 1867-1941. His sons Jack and Fred are sadly both deceased. Jack's son, John E., is still alive, as are his sons John E. and Mark, and another grandson, Peter Friend. All of the youngest generation are competent coracle-handlers.

Coracle Usage

At the time that Hornell was writing about (which was probably no later than the second world war) the coracle tradition in the Shrewsbury section of the Severn was being maintained, but only on a casual basis, and in the form of rod-and-line fishing, partly as a pastime and partly for a modest profit. In the 1980s the Davies family used their coracles in this manner. They maintained that as long as they were away from the bank they could fish anywhere on the Severn, providing they were not attached to the bank, because there was a free right of passage on the Severn. To do this, however, they accepted they had to have a lawful point of access such as at the Isle, where they were given the right to embark by the Holloways from the field belonging to their farm.

Fig 2 : 4
Three generations of the Davies family, traditional Shrewsbury coraclemen
L. to r.: Fred, Jack, John E, John, Mark.

Fig 2 : 5
A Shrewsbury coracle and coracleman in 1892.

Fig 2 : 6
A coracle in use in Phoenix Passage, Shrewsbury, during the 1936 floods.

Eel Night Lines

The laying of night lines for the catching of eels was practised using Shrewsbury coracles in the process certainly as late as the 1980s. The technique, according to John E. Davies, was very similar to that practiced at Ironbridge.

Firewood and Grafting Stocks

Jack Davies told the writer how during the Depression he and other coraclemen would take their coracles up-river to collect driftwood, which they then converted into firewood and sold on the doorstep in Shrewsbury to make ends meet.

Brian Waters describes being told by two coraclemen, William and Impy Bryan, who were reputed to make the strongest Shrewsbury coracles on the Severn, that they would go up-country by coracle searching for briars, which they would sell as grafting stocks to the Shrewsbury nurserymen.

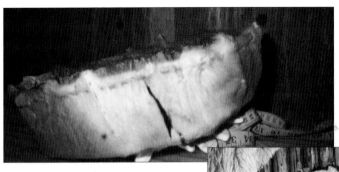

Plate 1:
Old bull boat, North Dakota Heritage Centre

Plate 2:
Replica bull boat at Knife River, North Dakota

Plate 3:
Replica bull boat made and being paddled by Terry Kenny,
the Ironbridge coracle-maker, c. 1989

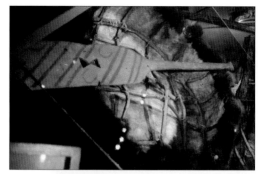

*Plate 4:
Bull boat paddle seen
at North Dakota
Heritage Centre in
1999*

*Plate 5:
William Rogers, of the Rogers family of Ironbridge, in an Ironbridge coracle
(date and artist unknown)*

Plate 6:
Coracles taking part in the Ironbridge Regatta, 2005

Plate 7:
Terry Kenny, a modern Ironbridge coracleman, on the Teifi at Cenarth,
in an Ironbridge coracle

Plate 8:
An Ironbridge coracle made by Eustace Rogers in the 1980s (author on left)

Plate 9:
A Bridgnorth coracle which is in the Bridgnorth Museum

Plate 10:
A forty-year-old Shrewsbury coracle made by Jack Davies

Plate 11:
The first Regatta at Leintwardine on the river Teme (1990s). Second from right: Dr. Geraint Jenkins, then President of the Coracle Society, is speaking; far right: Peter Faulkner.

Plate 12:
Peter Faulkner, former Chairman of the Coracle Society, at Cenarth in his Teme coracle

Plate 13:
Eustace Rogers of Ironbridge with a hide coracle he made in the 1980s

Plate 14:
A replica Scottish curragh made in 1996 by Olivia Elton Barratt, Mary Butcher,
Peter Faulkner (pictured) and the author

Plate 15:
The replica Scottish curragh under construction

Plate 16:
A Donegal paddling curragh
made by Andy McGonagle in
1992

Plate 17:
The Donegal paddling curragh
made for the author by Andy
McGonagle being launched in 1993

Plate 18:
Two Donegal curraghs in choppy
seas, 1992

Plate 19:
A Teifi coracle at the Cenarth Regatta in 1990

Plate 20:
A static Teifi coracle made by Ronald
Davies in 1986 for the author

Plate 21:
Reinforcing band on Teifi coracle
(c. 1994)

Plate 23:
Ronald Davies of Cenarth, a
traditional Teifi coracle-maker,
in 1990

Plate 22:
A Teifi coracle made by Bernard
Thomas of Llechryd in 1981

Plate 24:
A Teifi coracle being used in sheep-dipping at Cenarth Falls (date unknown)

Plate 26:
A fibre-glass Tywi coracle made by
Raymond Rees in the early 2000s

Plate 25:
A traditional Tywi coracle made by
Raymond Rees of Carmarthen for the
author (1980s)

Plate 27:
Edgworth Evans of St Clears at Cenarth in 1990

Plate 28:
Salmon Fishery: A view from the rocks of Aberystwith and the bay of
Aberystwith: *J. Hassell (1798).*

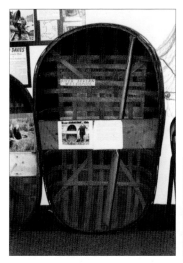

Plate 29:
*Replica Welshpool (upper Severn)
coracle, in the National Coracle Centre,
Cenarth*

Plate 30:
*Original Dwyryd coracle donated by the
author to the Museum of Welsh Life*

59

Plate 31:
An Indian coracleman sitting on an
upturned biscuit tin, river Cauvery area,
1994

Plate 32:
A coracleman near the river
Tunghabadra, India, 1994

Plate 33:
Vietnamese coracle, 2001

Plate 34:
Coracles in
Vietnam, 2001

Plate 35:
A coracle with
in-board engine
attached, Danang
area, Vietnam, 2001

Plate 36:
Vietnamese coracle with a number of supporting laths, Danang area, 2001

Plate 37:
Coracles carried on larger vessel, Nha Trang, 1994

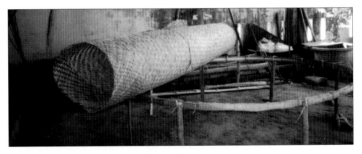

Plate 38:
Construction of a Vietnamese coracle: rolled mat on supported gunwale,
Danang, 2001

Plate 39:
Construction of a Vietnamese coracle: mat being 'kicked' into shape. Danang, 2001

Plate 40:
Finished Vietnamese coracle, showing two different patterns of weave

Plate 41:
Finished Vietnamese coracle, showing gunwale

Plate 42:
The author with Dwyryd coracle

Transportation

It will be recalled that one of the commonest coracle usages of the Ironbridge coracles was to enable people to cross the Severn from one bank to the other to get to and from work. Brian Waters told that at least one Shrewsbury coracleman used his craft to travel in this way on a regular basis. He was a man by the name of Thomas Powell.

Recovery of Footballs from the Severn

Reference will be made later in more detail to the practice of recovering footballs from the Severn by a coracleman, the late Fred Davies. In 1935 Hornell was told of a similar practice in relation to cricket balls on the Wye for the benefit of the Bishopswood and District Cricket Club.

Poaching

Jack Davies told me that in his early days when there was great unemployment and hardship, he and others used their coracles regularly for poaching. His coracle (Plate 10) and paddle were painted black. When they were on the river they often communicated by a system of signals consisting of different knocks on their coracles, and all called each other 'Mick'. It was clear from what I was told that they were nothing like modern poachers, and they had a deep concern for the countryside, which I witnessed on a number of occasions.

The Coracles

A consideration of the Ironbridge coracle as a coracle is relatively easy. Although they may have differed slightly in size to accommodate the relative size of the proposed user, in shape and method of construction they were virtually identical, unlike the Shrewsbury coracles. It will be seen from a comparison of the following coracles that there are marked differences. The old Shrewsbury coracle which belonged to Mrs J. F. Parker of Bewdley is on the same general pattern as the Welshpool (Welsh Severn) one, in contrast with modern Shrewsbury practice, where laths were laid on top of other laths, in having all the laths interlaced. The old and modern Shrewsbury coracles, however, differ between themselves in certain peculiarities. The chief of these are:

(a) The diagonal laths are complete, whereas they are reduced to short corner splints in [the modern Shrewsbury coracle].
(b) No accessory splints strengthen the bottom.

Hornell believes that a Welshpool coracle could well have been commonplace in those parts of the Severn where net fishing took place in the past, i.e. on the Welsh Severn. His view that it is similar to those used on the Wye and Usk areas does not seem tenable when a visual comparison is made, and regard is had to the fact that they, unlike the Welshpool and 'Mrs Parker's Shrewsbury Coracle' do not have woven gunwales, as do the Wye and Usk coracles.

Fig. 2:7 is a coracle made by the late Fred Davies in 1987, and to be seen at the Museum of Welsh Life. Its laths and gunwale are made of ash, covered by calico impregnated with pitch and tar. Its dimensions are length: 129 cm; width: 96 cm; and depth: 30 cm..

Fig. 2:8 is a coracle made for me in the 1980s by John E. Davies (son of Jack Davies senior). It is a more sturdy and larger craft, with wider laths and much deeper depth.

Fig. 2:9 is quite different from the coracles referred to above. It is currently in the Museum of Welsh Life. Hornell states that 'This is a comparatively modern modification devised about sixty years ago by the late Mr. H. Hudson, a Shrewsbury boat builder. It is characterised by the strong tumble-home of the sides due to the prominence of the bilge curve into which the bottom expands. This curious shape is obtained by the use of an elaborate wooden mould around which the framework is built ...'

It should be observed, in passing, that the prominence of the bilge curve is not dissimilar to that found in a Teifi coracle. It would undoubtedly make this coracle much more stable than a conventional Shrewsbury coracle.

Just after the Second World War an unusual coracle drifted down the Severn, and was recovered by the late Eustace Rogers from the Severn at Ironbridge. He believes it to be a Shrewsbury coracle. Although it is a little wider than an average Shrewsbury coracle, it is of a typical length and depth, and similar to the type made for me by John E Davies Also the laths are nailed on top of each other rather than interlaced. Most importantly there is a hole on the right of the seat. This clearly would have been used to house a rod and line when

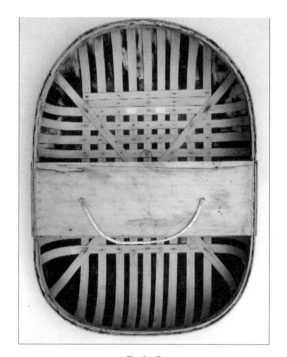

Fig 2 : 7
Coracle made by the late Fred Davies in 1987.

Fig 2 : 8
A Shrewsbury coracle made for the author by John E. Davies in the 1980s.

Fig 2 : 9
A Shrewsbury coracle made on a mould – currently in the Museum of Welsh Life.

not in use. As already mentioned, rod-and-line fishing was an important use of Shrewsbury coracles.

The first set of coracles constructed on the pioneering coracle-making courses at both the Greenwood Trust (now known as the Greenwood centre) and Bewdley Museum were made on the first course, under the guidance of the late Fred Davies. It is interesting to note that a Shrewsbury coracle was the craft chosen in the 1980s for this course. This was doubtless due to the fact it is probably the easiest coracle for a beginner to make, in that the overall shape does not call for an intricate woven gunwale, nor are the bends in the laths at all pronounced.

Whereas ash is always used to make Shrewsbury coracles, Brian Waters recalled being told by the Bryan brothers that briar made a good coracle.

Jack Davies also told me that he remembers coracles being made in the Shrewsbury area from briars, using a technique more akin to that used by the Boyne curraghmen of Ireland: namely, to construct the coracle from the gunwale upwards, as opposed to bottom upwards as the method used in all other coracles.

Finally it should be noted that Shrewsbury is the only town in which it was possible to buy a coracle from a shop, as Fig. 2:10 shows.

T. H. Williams' shop is specifically referred to by Waters, who states:

> A feature of Shrewsbury market that has gone was the shop of Williams, the net- and coracle-maker in Meadow Place ... Coracles at twenty five shillings each (I have heard of them being made and sold for as little as twelve shillings) were put on market day outside the shop where they sold 'like hot cross buns' to farmers whose land was fringed with meres, and a few were even sent abroad to customers in America and Australia. They were built, like many Shrewsbury coracles, on a frame ... Father and son could make a coracle a day, at the end of which was the job of covering the calico with tar and pitch, a hot, sunny day being chosen to drive the mixture home. This trade of net- and coracle-making was carried on by the Williams family for three hundred years, until salmon netting was prohibited.

For many years, the most common use of Shrewsbury coracles for fishing was by anglers using rod and line, but an eighteenth-century engraving shows, amongst other things, coracles with a net between them on the Severn at Shrewsbury. A copy of this engraving appears in a 1994 publication by Michael Rowe entitled *Shropshire in Pictures*.

W. Yarrell, writing in 1836, says that 'long doubly walled trammel nets are now in use near Shrewsbury'. This is the type of net traditionally used by coracle net fisherman on the Rivers Teifi and Tywy in west Wales. What is particularly interesting is the reference to the frequency of coracles made on a frame during the period Waters was writing about. This tends to support what Hornell said about the Shrewsbury coracle currently in the Museum of Welsh Life, but what is not clear is whether they had the Teifi style of 'a tumble-home'. In any event it was clear from my conversations with the Davieses that by no means all Shrewsbury coracles were made on a wooden mould.

The Davies family, traditional Shrewsbury coraclemen

Reference has already been made to this family. With the exception of James, who died in 1941, it has been my good fortune to have known James' sons Jack (John E Davies Senior) and Fred; Jack's son, John; and John's sons, John and Mark. I coracled with all of them except Fred. They were all accomplished coraclemen, and the elder

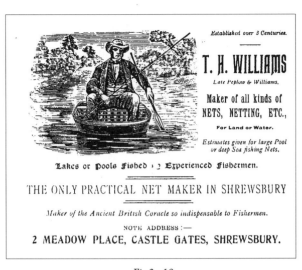

Fig 2 : 10
Advertisement for T. H. Williams' shop in Castle Gates, Shrewsbury.
Date unknown.

generation were also skilled coracle-makers. All of them were knowledgeable and responsible countrymen.

I clearly recall an occasion when I was on the Severn in the area of the Isle with Jack, his son John, and grandsons John and Mark. The river was in full spate. I got round without incident solely due to their collective skills. En route, a sheep was encountered which had fallen from an adjoining field onto a narrow ledge. It had panicked and become totally ensnared by brambles. John managed to get to the side, where his coracle was held steady by his sons whilst he climbed up the bank, cut the animal free, and literally threw it back to the field and safety. Without that exceptional skill in handling a coracle in fast-flowing waters and the use of considerable physical strength, the sheep would surely have died, as it would not have been visible to anyone in the field above. Mention of Jack has already been made earlier in this chapter. He belonged to the old school of coraclemen, but he gave very strong support to his son when the latter began making coracles in quantity and giving displays all over the country.

Fred Davies is probably the best known of all the family, due to his exploits when recovering footballs from the Severn for Shrewsbury Town Football Club. He was also well-known as the instructor to the enthusiasts who started the pioneering coracle-making courses at the Greenwood Trust and Bewdley Museum, referred to earlier.

Whilst Jack Davies was the most knowledgeable coracleman in the family, and Fred the best known, John Davies was the most prolific coracle-maker. Besides the traditional Shrewsbury coracle he made many other types. He made several different types of coracles for me, which are now in the National Coracle Centre at Cenarth, West Wales. John Davies was sufficiently highly regarded to have been asked to assist the local Coroner in Shrewsbury as an Expert Witness when a fisherman, Eddie Dineley of Merseyside, died on 3 April 1988 when attempting to use a coracle. It is profoundly to be hoped that the youngest generation of the Davies family will maintain the family reputation in the world of coracle-making.

Shrewsbury is particularly notable because it is the only place in England where a traditional coracle family remains now that Eustace Rogers of Ironbridge has died. It also has a rich heritage of coracle use, as shown by its having had a shop where coracles were routinely sold, the Frankwell coracle anglers, and Fred Davies' football retrieval skills.

BEWDLEY CORACLES

In common with Shrewsbury and Ironbridge, Bewdley does have a coracle tradition. Unlike them, however, it no longer continues the old tradition, although other coracles have been and are still being made in the town, through the good offices of Bewdley Museum.

The coracle itself
Bewdley coracles were oval in shape, as Mrs J. F. Parker told James Hornell. They were made in different shapes, those of average dimensions having six or seven longitudinal laths interlaced with ten transverse laths. One of their distinguishing features was that unlike any other coracle the frame was made of cleft oak, of which there was an abundance locally due to the proximity of the Wyre forest and the presence of tan pits in the town. Hornell said that another unusual

feature was that in order to carry the coracle on his back, the Bewdley coracleman used to insert the end of his paddle into a socket or shoe nailed to the bottom below the front edge of the seat, 'an alternative to the thong loop used at Ironbridge and Shrewsbury.' Nowhere else has such an arrangement been encountered.

The third significant feature is that although the covering used for the last-made coracles consisted of old sail cloth, impregnated with pitch and tar, it was not long ago that animal hide was used for covering their frames. No other English or Welsh coracle has used this method of covering recently (except the Teme coracle, of which more later). The reason for this can possibly be found in the presence of the tan pits, which would have been a ready source of supply of spoiled skins which could easily have been sewn up. Hornell records that one particular Bewdley family of coraclemen used to reinforce the frames of their coracles with strips of green hide. When these strips became dry, they both strengthened the lath framework and held its members in place 'as though bound with iron bands'.

The average length of the Bewdley coracle was 4' 9", and its width was 3' 7".

Usage

According to Hornell, they were used for 'ferrying, angling, laying lines and the carriage of stone and brick sinkers ... required for lines and putcheons employed in eel fishing'. He also said their width was probably accounted for by the fact they were used for carrying people across the Severn, in much the same way as Ironbridge coracles were used. He gives an example where four people were transported across the river by an elderly Bewdley coracleman. According to Mr F. Fisher (referred to in Hornell) the last coracle was made in Bewdley in 1908. The *Kidderminster Times* of the second June 1972, however, whilst agreeing with the last date of manufacture, goes on to say that they were still in use for some time after that.

The same paper describes a particularly gruesome use of coracles in the Bewdley area. It reads: 'A less salubrious use of the coracle involved the disposal of unwanted babies. They were set adrift in the craft at Bewdley bridge and floated downstream. At Redstone Rocks they were rescued by the hermits living there. The children were then reared in the 'community' under the name 'Severn'. Happily this custom died out long ago.'

The 'Stanley' coracle

In the Bewdley Museum is an unusual coracle. It almost certainly could not be termed a Bewdley coracle, in view of the nature of its construction. Considerable uncertainty surrounds it, but it would appear from correspondence involving the Museum and a Mr. R. Barker of Derby in May 1982 that it was made by a man named Stanley. He was not a native of Bewdley but lived in Kidderminster. He died in the late 1970s. He was very reluctant to be interviewed, but a local informant believed that Mr Stanley had ceased making coracles by the early 1940s.

It is Mr Barker's view (and he writes with evident knowledge) that the coracle in the Museum was built for fishing, for two people at a time. He says that his opinion is reinforced by the evident quality of its finish. In addition, its small 'fore deck' is not to be found in any other coracle, but would be very useful to a rod and line fisherman who spent long periods fishing from the craft.

That it can comfortably carry two people I can personally testify, having taken a freelance photographer in it on the Severn when he was photographing at a Bewdley regatta in the 1980s.

Contemporary coracles at Bewdley

Bewdley's first-ever regatta in modern times was held on the Severn at Bewdley in 1987. It was the brainchild of Charles Fogg, a Bridgnorth man, and the then Curator of Bewdley Museum. He started and ran the very popular and highly successful coracle-making courses at the Museum for a number of years, and his contribution to the revival of interest in coracles can not be overstated. Sadly, he and the Museum parted company, and for a time there was little coracle activity. Fortunately, the museum's technician in Charles Fogg's time, Dave Derby, remained, and he and Graham Fisher, a coracle enthusiast, have devoted themselves to building a collection of different types of coracles for the Museum.

TEWKESBURY CORACLES

Graham Hickman, an Ironbridge photographer and long-time resident who was a close neighbour of the late Eustace Rogers, told me that he was told by an elderly lady from Madeley Wood, who used to make nets for poachers, that there were coracles on the Severn at Tewkesbury which were of a different design to any other coracle found in the area. No more information has been forthcoming in relation to Tewkesbury coracles.

Thus it will be seen that the English Severn has a very rich coracling heritage.

TEME CORACLES

Two of the aims of the Coracle Society are the preservation of the way of life of those who make and use coracles in the traditional way, and the creation of interest in coracles in areas which do not have a significant coracle tradition. There was no tradition of coracle usage on the Teme in living memory, although the Teme coracle-maker, Peter G. Faulkner's grandfather, used a coracle in Ludlow which Faulkner believes was probably a Severn coracle. He said also that he had heard a story locally of someone in a coracle at Leintwardine in the 1920s. Leintwardine, the most northerly village in Herefordshire, is situated 9 miles west of Ludlow on the A 4113. Here the beautiful river Teme, spanned by a fine stone bridge, flows on its 85-mile journey to join the Severn below Worcester. In Leintwardine lived and worked Peter G. Faulkner, formerly Chairman of the Coracle Society, and a very successful coracle-maker and user.

In 1987, wishing to travel the length of his beloved Teme, he decided the best way to accomplish this was to build himself a coracle. At the time, Eustace Rogers was building hide-covered coracles as well as the traditional Ironbridge craft. Eustace told me he did this in an attempt to show what he believed the first coracles would have looked like. It was this hide coracle, which was constructed of 100% sustainable natural materials, which appealed to Peter Faulkner. In 1987 he visited Eustace and photographed one of his hide coracles, and also made a number of line drawings of it. Having also been given wise advice and sound instruction, he returned to Leintwardine where he made his first of many Teme Coracles. In it he travelled the full length of the Teme. Later he was to travel along the Severn, Wye, Thames and Shannon in a similar fashion: a total distance of well over 400 miles. From this early start he began to make a number of Teme coracles, many of which he sold to people all over the country. Many of his purchasers, however, were local people such as the Vicar, who blessed the first Leintwardine coracle regatta, and the butcher who supplied Peter with cow hides. Peter started annual coracle regattas at Leintwardine on the Teme during the 1990s, which were well-attended by coracle-paddlers and spectators (Plate 11).

Later Peter made a number of modified Boyne curraghs. (The original Boyne curragh will be dealt with fully in Chapter Three.) Finally he turned his hand at producing a number of hide covered curraghs. In one of these, Peter and others travelled from Ballycastle in Northern Ireland to Iona in June 1997.

It is interesting to compare a Teme coracle being paddled by Peter Faulkner (Plate 12), with a hide coracle made by Eustace Rogers (Plate 13). They are very similar in appearance, but not identical. The Teme coracle is slightly larger and more robust. Another difference is to be found in the respective lashings; Eustace used strips of hide, whereas Peter's are of horsehair.

Peter Faulkner said that it takes him about fifty hours to complete a Teme coracle. As will be seen, it is virtually bowl-shaped and consists of a frame of hazel sticks with a gunwale and floor of woven withy. It has five longitudinal and five transverse laths. They are neither sawn nor cleaved, and they are just over the thickness of a man's thumb. The seat, pillar and paddle are made of ash. Once completed, the frame, which has a diameter of approximately 4' 9" and a 14" depth, is covered with a single cowhide sewn on with horsehair cord. The hide is cured with a mixture of alum and salt petre, and waterproofed with lanolin. All the materials used are obtained locally.

It is no exaggeration to say that the contribution of Leintwardine, and particularly Peter Faulkner, to the continuance of interest in coracles has been immense.

AVON CORACLES

Hornell states his belief that coracles appear to have been used on
the Avon near Evesham in the seventeenth century. For this view he
relies on the writings of J. Aubrey, whom he quotes as saying 'The
boats on the Avon ... were baskets of twigs covered with an ox skin,
which the poor people of Wales use to this day, and call them
curricles'. Hornell goes on to say, 'Even today [presumably in the
1930s and 1940s] coracles are in use on this river near Evesham, but
it is a recent introduction, and is not the continuation of local
tradition so far as I know.'

He was clearly referring to coracle usage at Copthorne Mill,
Fladbury, Worcestershire, which is between Evesham and Pershore
and on the banks of the Avon. Here coracles are still used today. The
Mill was bought at the beginning of the twentieth century as a family
holiday home by the three brothers Louis, Harrison and Walter
Barrow. As at 1996, their descendants had, amongst a variety of craft
in the mill, some eight coracles.

Their first coracle was built by Louis Barrow in the 1880s
following his introduction to curraghs during a visit to Ireland. He
designed it for use as a tender to a steam launch he built. It also
doubled as a bath! On mooring for the evening it was filled with
water and heated by steam from the launch's boiler.

It was not, however, until 1926 that the first of the present range
of coracles was built. This followed a visit to the Rogers family at
Ironbridge. Apparently one of them found a coracle floating down
the Severn, restored it and sold it to Corbyn Barrow for half the price
he would have asked for one of his Ironbridge coracles, namely 30
shillings. It was used as a pattern for building subsequent coracles
and lasted a long time. I am indebted to Ben Barman, a senior
member of the Mill families, for this information. He was asked from
which of the Rogers family Corbyn Barrow had bought the coracle,
and made an enquiry from a very old member of the families, who
said he believed it to be Tommy Rogers. Tommy would have been
alive in 1926, but so would Harry and even Eustace; however, in view
of Tommy's leadership of the family it almost certainly would have
been him. It is a reasonable assumption that coracles built by
members of the families after 1926 would have closely resembled the

original coracle acquired from Tommy Rogers. Comparison of one of the subsequent coracles with that owned by Mrs Parker, referred to earlier, would suggest that the 1926 coracle was a Severn coracle emanating either from Shrewsbury or the area between Welshpool and Shrewsbury.

A particular favourite of the Mill is one made by Ben Barman in 1963. It is a good typical example of a modern Avon coracle. He described it to me as follows: 'Its dimensions are 54" x 38" x 15", which gives good stability and, at the same time, its weight happens to be a good balance between strength and lightness.'

Significant features of a typical 'Mill' Avon coracle are:
1. The laths are made of green oak
2. Small brass nuts and bolts are used to join the laths, rather than nails as were used in Severn coracles. The use of screws in this way makes repairs easier.
3. Ben Barman and others utilise materials used for boat covers which consist of cotton reinforced with abrasion-resistant synthetic fibre, in place of canvas as used hitherto. He pointed out that this material is waterproof, but he painted it with bitumastic paint in order to increase its life.

The 1926 and 1963 coracles played a significant part in the life of the Mill Families. This assertion is backed up by a correspondence I had with another senior member of the Families, David Livingstone of London, in 1990. He explained that it was the Families' tradition that before any young man married into the Families they had to make a coracle; a tradition he had personally observed.

The best-known Copthorne Mill coracle users today are Louis Barman, a descendant of the Families, and Christopher Sauvarin, who also has built a number of different types of coracle. He was an active committee member of the Coracle Society, and was for a number of years its Internet Education Officer.

WYE CORACLES

The next river to be considered is the Severn's beautiful sister, the Wye. Its proud tradition of coracle use came to an end with the

outbreak of the First World War. There are, however, many
references to coracles on the Wye in the many travel books written
about this river. James Hornell quotes from the 1760 edition of Izaak
Walton's *Compleat Angler*, in which Sir John Hawkins, describing his
piscatorial experiences on the Wye, indicates that it was not easy to
fish successfully without the use of a small boat. He writes:

> ... those of that country use a thing they call a *Thorrocle*, or *Truckle*;
> in some places it is called a *Coble*, from the Latin *Corbula*, a little
> basket: it is a basket shaped like half of a walnut-shell, but shallower
> in proportion, and covered on the outside with a Horse's hide: it has
> a bench in the middle, and will hold just one person, and is so light
> that the countrymen will hang it on their heads like a hood, and so
> travel with a small paddle which serves for a stick, till they come to a
> river: and then they launch it and step in: there is great difficulty in
> getting into one of these Truckles; for the instant you touch it with
> your foot, it flies from you, and when you are in, the least inclination
> of the body oversets it. It is very diverting to see how upright a man
> is forced to sit in these vessels, and to mark with what state and
> solemnity he draws up the stone which serves for an anchor, when
> he would remove, and lets it down again ...

This description is interesting for a number of reasons. The
description well describes the Wye coracle presently in the Museum
of Welsh Life (Fig. 2:11). No other coracle is specifically called a
'Truckle'. The 'Coble' found on the North East coast of England is a
totally different type of craft.

Finally, the reference to the use of a stone as an anchor would
suggest the Wye coracle observed by Hawkins would have been used
for rod and line rather than net fishing.

Hornell mentions next in chronological order, a description
contained in *Historical Tour through Monmouthshire, Brecon, 1904,*
wherein W. Coxe, who passed through Monmouthshire in 1799,
gives the following account:

> During the course of the navigation from Ross, we passed several
> small fishing craft, called Truckles or Corricles, ribbed with laths or
> basket work, and covered with pitched canvas. Like a canoe, the
> corricle holds only one person, who navigates it by means of a
> paddle with one hand, and fishes with the other; these boats are so
> light, that the fishermen throw them on their shoulders and carry
> them home.

Fig 2 : 11
A Wye coracle.

It is interesting that the craft is referred to as a Truckle or a 'corricle'. (The late Eustace Rogers in conversation always called all coracles 'corricles'.)

The description is also noteworthy in its reference to the craft being covered with 'pitched canvas'. It is one of the earliest references to the use of canvas as a cover for coracles, rather than flannel in west Wales or animal hide elsewhere.

Hornell quotes *Travels in Great Britain*, published in 1805, in which the Duke of Rutland describes seeing coracles being used on the Wye for fishing with nets. 'Each man lays hold of one end of a net, about 20 yards long, and paddles down the river, till they feel a strike. They then haul it up as quick as possible, and draw it on shore'. This account could easily be of net fishing on the rivers of west Wales today.

Bewdley Museum has in its possession an article on Wye coracles, author unknown, circa 1880. In it is this description of a nineteenth-century Wye coracle:

> It is in shape rather like a flat half-walnut shell, the frame of sticks or laths forming a sort of open lattice work, covered with canvas (or now sometimes zinc) instead of hide, with a plank across as a seat. It is propelled by a paddle, and is so light as to be carried with ease on the back. An inexperienced navigator will probably find it at first

better suited for putting him into than keeping him out of the water, as these 'cockle shells' are very crank.

The interesting thing about this description is the reference to zinc. The latest Llangollen (Dee) coracles were sometimes made also of aluminium laths. Moreover, fibreglass has also been used recently on the Teifi and Tywi, but this is the only reference to the use of zinc in coracles as a cover.

An unusual method of rod and line fishing on the Wye is given by Robert Pashly, who corresponded with Hornell in the 1930s, and is referred to by him. He wrote: 'others only had a large bung on a short piece of cord attached to the rod butt, and on hooking a fish the lot was heaved overboard. The rod etc, played the fish, and directly he rested the fisherman paddled after his bung and gave it a pull to start his quarry off again.'

This theme is enlarged, in a manner of speaking, in the July 1992 edition of *Country Quest*. In it (p. 39) reference is made to a tourists' guide book to South Wales written by a Mr and Mrs S. C. Hall in 1961. They wrote: 'Sometimes a little fleet of these tiny boats, peculiar to the district, may be seen here anchored up and down the rapids below New Weir, casting for Trout, Pink and Grayling. Many a salmon of size has thus been taken and carried to shore; and in the season it is not unusual for a fisherman to fill his coracle with the smaller fish of this bountiful river.' Coracle-fishers used a variety of ingeniously contrived gear to make their catches. The usual coracle rod was of elm 'stiff and shaped like a billiard cue with a very heavy butt'. The line was made of horsehair, and was tapered .

Another truckle fisher, who had retired from the GWR after fifty years service, and who lived at Kerne Bridge, 'used a reel, but others had a large cork bung on a piece of cord attached to the rod butt, and on hooking a fish the lot was heaved overboard. The rod etc played the fish.'

It is difficult to deduce the period they were writing about, but it certainly could not have been the 1960s. It is suggested it probably was the period written about by Robert Pashley, who was describing the Wye before the First World War.

It will be apparent that some of the references to coracles on the Wye refer to the Welsh section of that river. They have have nevertheless been included because there is no difference in design or function between the Wye coracles found in Wales and England and, in any event, certain areas such as Monmouth over the years have sometimes been regarded as being in Wales and sometimes in England. It is submitted that it would be artificial to exclude all references to Wye coracles in Wales in a consideration of the English Wye coracle, particularly in view of the length of the English Wye.

William Dew and the Wye coracle

William Dew of Kerne Bridge was probably the best-known Wye coracleman. He died in 1933. During his life, 'he fished for trout and coarse fish for years after he finished salmon fishing.' So wrote Hornell. Within the same page it is suggested that one of the Phelps' family fished for salmon after Dew, but predeceased him. There is in the Hereford County Museum a Wye coracle made by William Dew not later than 1880, and which, according to A. V. Lucas (*Romantic Symbols of the Wye Valley, c.*1948), he used until 1910.

Hornell had a model Wye coracle made for him which he gave to the Science Museum in London (Fig. 2:12). It was made by a former Wye coracleman, A. C. Morgan of Monmouth. It is interesting to note that the Morgan model shows more clearly than the Dew coracle that the gunwale is joined by lashings such as are to be found in Boyne and Spey curraghs. It will also be seen that the shape of the Wye coracle quite closely resembles Teifi and Tywi coracles. Moreover, the paddle is similar to a Tywi paddle, being of considerable length.

Coracle Races

Most coracle rivers had races, and the Wye was no exception. A. C. Morgan told Hornell that special coracles were made for racing: noticeably longer than fishing coracles, and both ends were alike and well rounded. The making of coracles specifically for racing was not unknown on other rivers.

Allied to this was the possible use of coracles for long journeys on the Wye. There is no suggestion that coracles were specially made or adapted for such voyages. Instances of men travelling from Ross or Chepstow are mentioned by Hornell.

The Coracle Society Newsletter dated June 1993, in its section

Fig 2 : 12
Model of a Wye coracle made by A. C. Morgan of Monmouth for James Hornell,
and given by Hornell to the Science Museum in London.

'From the River Bank' refers to a journey made by Luke Hughes of Wilton, who paddled his truckle to Lundy Island some three hundred years ago.

Modern Wye coracle usage

The Independent dated 14 September 1987 showed a picture of William Teiser of Bulls Hill in a coracle made by Ricky Howells, formerly of Ross on the River Wye. In 1992, Tim Oakes, then a radio reporter, built a replica Wye coracle. In 1995 he was visited by a writer for *The Times*, Clive Fewins, and a photographer, who spent a day with him discussing Wye coracles. This resulted in an article appearing in *The Times* (15 April 1995) headed 'Vision of a Coracle Armada'. As a result Oakes received many enquiries from far and wide for Wye coracles.

RIVERS OR AREAS WHERE OTHER CORACLES ARE OR WERE FOUND

Coracles are now made in at least two areas which have no tradition of coracle manufacture or usage. They are Cornwall and Norfolk.

Cornwall

Michael Ransley, a self-taught coracle-builder with considerable woodworking skills, ran courses in coracle-making at Lanlivery in

Cornwall. The coracles when completed were launched on a nearby river at Lostwithiel.

Norfolk

One of the contributors to this book, Conwy Richards, a recent Chairman of the Coracle Society, lives in Wereham, Kings Lynn, in Norfolk. In addition to running a prolific website focusing on coracles, he builds many coracles of varied types, and makes coracle nets.

Thames

Unlike Cornwall and Norfolk, there is some evidence to suggest a coracle tradition on the River Thames. This evidence, it is accepted, is tenuous. It consists of the following:

1. In the 1980s or 1990s I had a conversation with the then technical adviser to the Worshipful Company of Basket Makers, who had served his apprenticeship with a firm of Charing Cross Basket Makers, G. W. Scott and Sons. They were formed in 1669, but are no longer in business. He said that their trade mark contained a coracle. (To date it has not been possible to establish the existence of this trade mark.)
2. The well-documented account (in Hornell, for example) of a race between a Thames waterman and a Spey curragh man on the Thames in London to settle a wager between an English aristocrat and a Scottish laird, which will be described in Chapter Three.
3. The observations of the well respected historian, Christopher Hibbert MC, in his book *London, the Biography of a City* (1969). He states that coracles were in evidence on the river during the building of a second bridge over the Thames in the city. He writes: 'Yet the building of a second bridge further upstream was constantly opposed both by the City ... and by the powerful company of watermen who made their living by plying the fleet of wherries, coracles ... that filled the river at all hours', and also speaks of 'the poor fishermen, whose only possessions were their coracles and tackle'. The location of these coraclemen would appear to have been in the vicinity of the current London Bridge. (I corresponded with Hibbert in March 1998. Despite being

most helpful and courteous, he was unable to say what the source of this information was. It is submitted, however, that it is very unlikely that such a respected and careful historian would have made these statements without a sound basis for doing so.)

It is hoped that from what has been written it will be seen what a rich coracling heritage England has, and that the vibrant new interest in coracles in England bodes well for the future of coracles and those who use them.

Notes

1 J. H. B. Peel, *Portrait of the Severn* (Robert Hall Ltd, 1968), p. 36
2 Geraint Jenkins, *The Coracle* (David & Charles Ltd, 1988), p. 110
4 S. Smith, *A View from the Ironbridge* (1979), p. 17
4 A J Mugridge, Coracles, *Miners and Other Memories* (1997)
5 Wilfred Byford-Jones, *Severn Valley Stories* (Shropshire Star & Journal, 1967), p. 90
6 Brian Waters, *Severn Stream* (J. M. Dent & Sons Ltd, 1949), p. 136

Chapter Three
SCOTTISH AND IRISH CURRAGHS

Coracles and allied craft were not confined to England and Wales, and areas beyond Europe such as India, Vietnam and Tibet, but were also to be found in Scotland and Ireland. Whereas English coracles are very different in shape and purpose to Scottish and Irish curraghs, a Scottish curragh (Plate 19) and the Ironbridge coracle have a very similar shape, as will become apparent when the Scottish curragh is examined and the Ironbridge coracle recalled. Hornell, referring to the Ironbridge coracle points out that 'a less clumsy model of coracle is required than that favoured by salmon fishers; some stability has to be sacrificed to speed and manoeuvring power. As a result the design has become stabilised in the form of a shallow oval bowl'.

In his article 'The Curragh in Scotland' in *A Journal of the School of Scottish Studies* (1972), Alexander Fenton remarks: 'Just as the men of Ironbridge on the Severn used a coracle in the shape of a shallow, oval bowl where great manoeuvrability was required, for example when catching rabbits marooned during floods, so the similar shape of the only surviving Scottish curragh may be due to a comparable need in relation to the floating of timber.' Having used both craft on a number of occasions, I can confirm that they are both more manoeuvrable and less stable than a number of British types of coracle, because the shallow shape promotes speed but the lack of tumble-home produces less stability.

It is suggested, therefore, that Scottish curraghs should now be considered in some detail.

Hornell in his writings refers to the Scottish craft as a coracle. It would seem from a linguistic standpoint such a practice is incorrect, the word 'coracle' having its origins in the Brythonic branch of the Celtic language, and the curragh in the Goidelic branch. Having said this, the logic in Hornell's terminology from a pragmatic point of view is undeniable. It is beyond argument that the shape, construction and usage of the Scottish and Boyne curraghs is more akin to coracles than seagoing curraghs, which are essentially boat-shaped craft, for the most part. Although coracles such as the Towy and Teifi versions are used in tidal waters, in general coracles are essentially inland craft.

In addition to the Scottish and Boyne curraghs, the Owey Island (Donegal) curragh will be considered, as it can be regarded as the missing link between coracles and curraghs.

SCOTTISH CURRAGHS

In *British Coracles and Irish Curraghs*, Hornell asserts that 'Notices of the use of coracles in Scotland are of the scantiest, but what there are possess vivid human interest.' It is true that there is only one surviving specimen of this very interesting type of coracle, which was probably used on the Spey in connection with the timber trade, but there is evidence that curraghs were in use in other parts of Scotland. What is far from clear, however, is whether they were all of a similar design, or varied as in England and Wales.

Fenton writes: '... nevertheless information about the form and construction of the craft is not found in legal records; and while drawings of coble-fishing scenes appear in Slezer's *Theatrum Scotiae* of 1693, he has no view of the Spey, and in no case does a curragh appear in his engraved views.'

With some reluctance it is submitted that Hornell's contribution to a study of the Scottish Curragh does not measure up to the high standard he reaches when considering other forms of coracle or curragh. This will become apparent when the construction of the curragh is dealt with later, but also when identifying historical references to Scottish curraghs.

Historical references
These are to be found in the works of Hornell and Fenton. The latter states that '... documentary evidence begins to appear in the fifteenth century and runs till the end of the eighteenth century.' Hornell, on the other hand claims – incorrectly, as it will be seen – that 'the earliest record is a racy account by Hector Boece, who wrote in 1527.' Fenton's references are as follows:

1. 1487: a grant of net fishing rights by curragh on the Spey.

2. Early sixteenth-century entries in the Rental of Dunkeld diocese describe the use of curraghs for fishing on the Tay.

3. Purchases of curraghs, and hides; also 'barking and fitting' in 1508-9, 1510, and 1511. (The location is not mentioned but it is obviously in Scotland, presumably in the Tay area.)

4. 1527: an account of the appearance and use of curraghs in the Highlands, mentioned by Hornell. Referring to it Fenton states: 'Here are assembled the characteristic features of the curragh used on inland waters: the structure of hide and wands, the method of transport on the back, along with its common functions of fishing and ferrying.'

5. 1542: a grant by the Bishop of Moray to a son of the chief of Grant to fish with curraghs on the Spey.

6. 1569 and 1586: more references to fishing by curragh.

7. 1594: a record of curragh fishing in Glendochart relating to the loan to a neighbour by a McNab (in Innishewan) of a 'currok and other graith [gear] to slay the red fisch ...' Fenton concludes: 'From the contexts of these references, it can be seen that fishing was carried on in the lochs and rivers by estate fishermen using curraghs and hempen nets, as well as with hooks and lines.' The reference to 'hempen' nets is interesting when, as will be seen later, horse hair was used in the construction of the surviving curragh. Moreover, until very recently nets were made exclusively of either horse or cow hair by the coracle net fishermen of west Wales.

8. 1617: a reference to the right to fish on the Spey for salmon by curragh.

9. 1684: a similar reference.

10. 1705: a similar reference.

11. 1778: a recognition by the Court of Session of the right of the Earl of Fife to fish with curraghs.

12. 1798: a letter written by the Reverend Doctor John Bethune, born in Kintail in 1746, dated 22 May 1798, in which he stated that the curragh was formerly in widespread use in the Highlands as a ferry boat on rivers and small creeks. He also said that the 'courich was very commonly used' in the West Highlands of Ross-shire. In the same letter, Dr Bethune added that the curragh had been replaced by a 'sort of canoe called Ammir i.e. trough'.

Fenton considers it scarcely that the dug out canoe could have replaced the curragh and that 'of these two kinds of primeval vessel, the curragh disappeared a little earlier than the dug-out in the West Highlands, or at least in some parts of the region'.

12. The use of the curragh in connection with the floating of timber down the Spey will be dealt with separately. Suffice to say that 'by the opening of the eighteenth century' was the date that such usage started .

So far, consideration has been given to documentary history but, of course, oral tradition plays a very important part in tracing early coracle usage. Hornell rather inappropriately refers to it as 'fairies and second sight'; Fenton far more pertinently as 'Gaelic oral tradition'. They both speak of similar incidents but interpret them in very different ways. Where there is a difference, it is suggested that Fenton's assessment is the more reliable.

Fenton first relates to a prophesy attributed to a sixteenth-century seer known as 'Coinneach Odhar', in which the fairy flag of the clan MacLeod features. It indicates the availability of curraghs to ferry all gentlemen of the name of Macleod across Loch Dunvegan in Skye.

Another oral source given by Fenton seeks to depict how the fourth chief of Clanranald of Moidart seized the chief of the Mackintosh clan in Loch Moy in Eastern Inverness-shire. This would have been about the end of the fifteenth century. The importance of the reference is that it states that Clanranald 'had carried with him several boats of hides'. It is interesting to compare this with the use made of hide-covered craft by the Mandan Indians when attacking other tribes, as described in Chapter One.

The final incident cited by Fenton 'seems to establish for the Argyle area the wicker frame, the hide covering, and the one-man crew'. No date is mentioned, although the information apparently derives from John Paterson MacLean in his *History of the Isle of Mull.*

Curraghs and the Spey timber trade

Fenton states: 'By the opening of the eighteenth century a different use for the curragh, though apparently not very long-lived, had made its appearance in the records. This was in helping to guide logs or

88

sawn deals that were being floated down the Spey and its many tributaries'. The distance involved was between twenty and thirty miles.

The first reference to this practice mentioned by Hornell is dated 1730, on the occasion of the sale of the woods of Abernethy to the Yorkshire Buildings Company by the Laird of Grant. According to James Hornell, 'The company began operations on an extensive scale, but found great difficulty in rafting the timber without guidance down the turbulent waters of the Spey. To remedy this the following device was tried and found successful. A coracle, connected to a number of logs by a horsehair tow rope, went ahead to keep the raft straight, assisted by a man walking along the opposite banks with ropes attached to the after-end of the raft to check undue velocity and steer it'. According to P. Abernethy, the fore-end of the tow rope made a running knot or loop round the paddler's knees, 'so that if the raft stopped on a stone or any other way, he loosed the knot and let his curragh go on, otherwise it would sink in a strong stream; and, after coming in behind the raft again and loosing it, he proceeded again.'

Fenton's description of the technique used is basically the same as that given by Hornell, but he amplifies it by saying that the guiding rope may not always have been secured around the curragh man's knees but held in his hand, requiring the curragh to be paddled with the other arm. This, of course, is the technique used by the net fishermen of west Wales to this day, when fishing for salmon or sewin with a net held between two coracles. Fenton relies for this proposition on an account given by Shaw in 1775. This possibility of one-handed paddling will be of relevance when the construction of the curragh is considered later. I have paddled a replica curragh with one as well as two hands without any difficulty, and no problem would be experienced by holding a line in one hand whilst paddling the craft with the other.

Fenton, however, cites a letter from Castle Grant to the Earl of Findlater in 1701 which clearly describes the use of curraghs in guiding timber down the Spey. The account given is quite detailed and specifies the number of trees involved on two separate occasions and, interestingly, refers to the curragh being brought back from the mouth of the Spey on the back of the curraghman – a very coracle-like feature.

Neither Hornell nor Fenton provides any clear evidence of curraghs being used in connection with the transport of timber by river before the eighteenth century. Fenton, however, describes how the curraghs were superseded by timber rafts within a few years of 1728.

Hornell and Fenton, with good reason, have no doubt that the surviving Scottish curragh mentioned earlier, and which will be discussed later, was used in the transportation of timber on the Spey.

Whilst undoubtedly the life of a Spey curraghman must have been hard, it had its lighter moments. Both Fenton and Hornell refer to an account by Glenmore – a pseudonym – writing in *Highland Legends and Fugitive Pieces of Original Poetry, with translations from the Gaelic* (1859). The story relates that his chief, the Laird of Grant, was 'in company of English friends, admiring the shipping on the Thames, when one of the Englishmen said to the Laird: 'I suppose you have nothing like that on your puny Spey.' Grant's Highland pride was roused, and he retorted, 'I have a subject on the Spey who in a boat of bullock's hide, would outstrip any craft.' The Englishman smiled, and a money bet was made on the spot. The Laird of Grant undertook to have his man and the boat on the Thames on a certain day. The young man who volunteered ... took his curragh to London, and in the presence of a great crowd of spectators, the Strathspey man soon outpaced his rival in his light craft.'

James Hornell's account is substantially the same except that he specifies the finishing point, namely London Bridge. His information was derived from an old newspaper cutting supplied by W. E. Watson, the Honorary Secretary, Elgin and Morayshire Literary Association, but a date is not supplied for either the contest or the newspaper cutting. There can, however, be no doubt that Fenton and Hornell are writing about the same event.

In the absence of any information concerning the length of the race, the tidal conditions prevailing, or the type of craft used by the waterman, it is difficult to draw any firm conclusions from the accounts. Suffice it to say that the unusually broad paddle (much wider than any other coracle or curragh paddle) in the hands of a very strong and skilful man, as no doubt Spey curraghmen would have been, might explain how he was able to vanquish a Thames waterman if he were rowing a passenger-carrying wherry rather than a skiff.

THE ELGIN CURRAGH

Referring to Spey curraghs, Fenton states 'by the 1790s only one was known to survive in the Parish of Cromdale'. It is therefore remarkable that a single example of the curragh still remains in Scotland. Today it is housed in the Museum of the Elgin Society in Scotland. In the early twentieth century it was found under the rafters of his farm buildings in central Strathspey by a Mr. Grant, Mains of Advie, Morayshire, who presented it to the Museum.

Fig. 3:1 shows a view of the curragh with its seat and paddle. It will be seen that it appears to be virtually circular, which conforms to a number of descriptions of earlier Scottish curraghs, but the Reverend Lachlan Shaw, writing in 1775 in a *History of the Province of Murray – Edinburgh*, describes Spey curraghs as being 'as in shape oval, four feet long and nearly three broad, a small keel from head to stern, a few ribs across the keel, and a ring of pliable wood around the lip of it, the whole covered with a rough hide of an ox or horse. The coracleman sat on a transverse seat in the middle; if a passenger were taken, he stood behind the paddler, leaning on his shoulders'. A number of interesting points arise from this description:

Fig 3 : 1
A Spey curragh, showing seat and paddle, in Elgin Museum.

1. The shape is more oval than round. It will be recalled that whereas the current Ironbridge coracle built by the late Eustace Rogers is round, that built by his father, Harry Rogers, is distinctly oval. In any event there were many variants in the shape and size of a number of British coracles.
2. The reference to the use of horse or ox-hide as a covering is interesting and not replicated in English coracles.
3. So far as the occasional transportation of passengers is concerned, it will be recalled that a similar practice in relation to Bewdley coracles was described in Chapter Two.
4. Finally, the reference to a keel is striking. Hornell believes Shaw to be mistaken in his description. Fenton, however, whilst accepting that keels are non-existent in English and Welsh coracles, and even in curraghs generally, is reluctant to dismiss Shaw's description so summarily as, in Fenton's opinion, Shaw was a careful observer and lived at a time when Spey curraghs were in daily use. He suggests that possibly he was using the term 'keel' freely for an internal spar that ran fore and aft (i.e. a keelson) to give added support. (An examination of Vietnamese coracles, about which more will be said in a later chapter, will show that they have a 'basket-like frame' which is supported by independent external as well as internal laths.)

As has been mentioned, Hornell, for his description of the Elgin curragh, relied on a photograph and details supplied to him in 1935 by W. E. Watson, the then honorary curator of the Elgin Museum.

Alexander Fenton does not disagree with most of Hornell's description, but he corrects one part of it relating to the construction of the gunwale. This came about as the result of renovation work carried out by the National Museum of Antiquities of Scotland on the Spey curragh in 1970.

Hornell's description is as follows: 'This has a shallow bowl-shaped framework, oval in plan. It appears to have been wrought throughout of closely woven wickerwork, although almost the whole of the bottom is broken away. The exterior is covered with a strong bull hide, its edges reflected over the stout cylindrical gunwale. Its size is 5 feet long by 4½ feet beam. (The assistant Curator of Elgin Museum, Christine Sangster, measured the curragh for me on 6

October 1988, providing the following dimensions: diameter 1450 mm; paddle length 1150 mm; seat length 1140 mm/width 280 mm. From these measurements it would appear that the shape of the curragh has changed, perhaps due to its age, becoming more circular.) Hornell continues: 'A wooden seat is the full width of the coracle and 11 inches broad. Apart from two holes in each end through which passed cords or thongs, tying it in position, three round holes were present. Through two probably passed the ends of a carrying rope or thong. The significance of the third is not clear'.

Fenton, whilst agreeing that two of the holes could have been used as a carrying band, suggests that the third might have been used by the passing of one end of the carrying band through it, as well as the other two, thereby providing the opportunity for adjustment which the utilisation of two holes would not have permitted. When the Teifi coracle is considered in Chapter Four, it will be seen that three holes in its seat are used for the carrying band. The other possibility of housing a securing peg for a towing line was considered earlier.

Hornell states: 'As will be seen from an examination of the photograph, the technique of the framework is different from that of any existing Welsh or English coracle; it diverges equally from that of the Irish or Boyne type and approaches rather that of the guffas of Iraq. Instead of being comprised of two series of widely separated laths or pliant rods interlaced at right angles, the frame here is of true wicker basket-work'. (It is considered that the Vietnamese coracle is even nearer to the Spey curragh than the guffa of Iraq, as will be apparent when illustrations of both appear later and are compared.)

Hornell continues: 'The main ribs, the warp, are arranged in numerous closely-set pairs which radiated from and must have crossed what was the centre of the bottom, outwards to the gunwale periphery. On this many-rayed star the weft is woven in tightly packed concentric rings as in a wicker basket. It is notable that the paired warp units are made of slender withies of twig thickness similar to those forming the weft. The latter have been split before use, and generally those of the warp are also in the split condition. They appear to be of willow, and still retain the bark.'

So far as the description of the gunwale is concerned, that given by Alexander Fenton is preferred for the reasons already mentioned.

Correcting Hornell, he states: 'In fact the gunwale is formed of a single pliant rod whose maximum diameter is 2¼ inches with tapered ends overlapped over a distance of 47 inches across the cord of the ark, which is bound to the centre of the overlap by three lashings of slender withy, and a further two withy lashings grip the ends of the gunwale rod, making a total of five lashings. The lashings are formed by winding the withy round four or five times and tucking in the loose ends.'

Hornell concludes: 'The edge of the hide cover is turned over the gunwales and held in place by a continuous lacing of twisted horsehair cord; this passes in long loops through holes in the edge of the hide to points several inches below the gunwale on the inner side, where the cord of each loop is passed behind one pair of warp withies and then led back to the edge of the cover. The paddle (Fig. 3:2) is barely 4 feet in length. The blade is flat, broad and spade-shaped, 17

Fig 3 : 2
A Spey curragh paddle. Elgin Museum.

inches long by 11 inches in width. The loom, 2½ feet, is sub-cylindrical and 2 x 1¾ inches in cross section, with a straight cross-crutch at the top.'

The fact that the centre of the curragh had disintegrated posed problems for Fenton, who wrote: 'Unfortunately the lower part of the wicker frame is missing and there is no direct means of ascertaining fully it original appearance.' Moreover, he is critical of Hornell's proposition that all the warp withies crossed at the bottom, because if that is right, 'a lumpy and unworkmanlike bundle would have been produced.' He suggests that 'either the basketwork frame did not extend all the way to the bottom or, more likely, a good number of the warps must have tapered off before reaching the bottom.'

Because of this dilemma, a representative of the Coracle Society (me), and members of the Basket Makers Association, joined together to build a replica Spey curragh. What was discovered during the construction process will be described next.

The building of a replica Spey Curragh

In April 1989 I joined a party of very experienced Basket Makers, including the then President of the Basket Makers' Association, Olivia Elton Barratt, and Mary Butcher, the trade advisor to the Worshipful Company of Basket Makers. Two replica Spey curraghs were made (Plate 14). They have both been used extensively and found to be wholly satisfactory. One is now in the National Coracle Centre, Cenarth, west Wales; the other is in the possession of Olivia Elton Barratt.

The Worshipful Company requested that a third replica be made for them. This was duly done by Olivia Elton Barratt and Mary Butcher with some small help from me. It was to all intents and purposes the same as the other two craft, but larger (Plate 15).

The question of possible support for the seat of the curragh is very interesting. All the British coracles past and present have seats, as do Boyne and Donegal curraghs. Coracles emanating from India, Iraq, North America and Vietnam, however, do not. British coracles are propelled by a single paddle from a sitting position. But the non-British coracles are paddled from a kneeling rather than a sitting position. It should be noted that the Boyne and Donegal curraghs require a seat to enable a second person to be carried in the curragh to handle nets, and also assist in guiding the craft with a second paddle.

The Spey curragh in size, shape and usage is similar to the Ironbridge coracle which, as has been described, is paddled by a single coracleman from a sitting position. Accordingly it seems very likely indeed that the Spey curragh had some form of seat support.

The first hides used on the two replicas were tanned and obtained, with some difficulty, from a traditional firm of tanners in South London. The reason that they were tanned is because that was what was used on Boyne Curraghs, the last known hide-covered coracles. Later, however, they were replaced by the hides. These were put on by Peter Faulkner, the Teme coracle-maker, all of whose craft are covered with animal hide. The Worshipful Company's curragh was similarly covered.

Finding anyone who would supply horse-hair line for lashing purposes proved to be very difficult. Eventually it was Peter who made and supplied it..

Finally, it should be said that the Spey curragh is one of the most interesting coracle-like craft – because of the nature of its construction and usage, but also because it is one of the last of the traditional craft to have ceased fishing in the time-honoured way.

BOYNE AND DONEGAL CURRAGHS

Before examining either of these in detail a number of matters arise.

Irish curraghs, in general, have a very long and interesting history. Kevin Danaher, a noted writer on Irish folk matters, referring to skin boats consisting of a light framework with a skin of thin material stretched over them, wrote in *Ireland's Traditional Crafts*: 'Their making is a tradition of such immense antiquity that there is no certainty as to how or when they originated, but they probably date from the waning Ice Age of the Upper Palaeolithic, some twenty thousand years ago'.

There are numerous accounts of epic voyages having been made by hide-covered craft; the legendary voyaging of St. Brendan in the sixth century being a prime example. Moreover, 'there is no doubt that the monks of the Irish church went far afield in their skin boats and almost certainly reached Iceland before the Norsemen' – so wrote Professor E. Estyn Evans in *Irish Folk Ways*.

When the word 'curragh' is used in conversation, what comes to mind is a picture of a boat substantially longer than it is wide, covered with hide, canvas or the like, and which is rowed rather than paddled – unlike the coracle which is round, oval- or kidney-shaped, and generally propelled by a single paddle.

For the sake of clarity, the type of curraghs described above will be referred to from here onwards as 'seagoing curraghs'.

I suggest that the craft that goes back to pre-history, and those in which were made those epic sea voyages earlier referred to, are these seagoing curraghs.

Hornell, in *The Curraghs of Ireland,* makes two significant historical references to Irish curraghs. Firstly, he quotes a translated entry in the *Annals of Ulster,* under the year 621 AD, referring to the drowning of Connaing, son of Aedhan mac Gabhrain of the Irish kingdom in Scotland, when the chronicler sings, 'The great clear waves of the sea and sand have covered them – into his frail wicker curragh they fling themselves over Connaing'. Secondly, he mentions the only early English record of curraghs, which is contained in the Anglo Saxon Chronicle and by Florence of Worcester. It describes how three pious Irish men landed in Cornwall in a hide-covered boat of the proportions of a small seagoing curragh in the year 891.

At the Coracle Society AGM in Bodnant Gardens, north Wales, on 17 June 2000, I had the briefest of conversations with a man who told me that he had seen single-seater curraghs propelled by a single paddle on the river Shannon near Jamestown. He was unable to say whether they were craft indigenous to the river Shannon or had been imported from the Boyne.

Some years earlier, also at an AGM this time in Llangollen, North Wales, I was told by a spectator, watching a coracle display on the river Dee, that he had seen 'round coracles' some three years earlier in County Meath. This is not so surprising, as there is clear evidence of Boyne coracles having been used in the vicinity of Slane castle, County Meath, in the twentieth century. These would have been used in the traditional way for the netting of salmon. Moreover, recently, there has been a revival in Boyne curragh manufacture and recreational, but not traditional, usage..

The paucity of information contained in these reports illustrates the problems encountered by the researcher into inland coracle-type craft – a difficulty not experienced when researching seagoing curraghs.

Seagoing curraghs are still to be found extensively along the west coast of Ireland. Their level of sophistication increases the further west one goes, culminating in the Kerry curragh, known locally as a 'Naomhog'. This craft has more than one pair of oars and sometimes carries, additionally, a sail.

None of these curraghs will be considered in this or any other chapter because they are rowed as opposed to paddled, occasionally sailed, and are essentially seagoing craft. This means that they do not come within the criteria referred to earlier when defining what, in practice, amounts to a coracle-type craft.

There are, however, two types of curragh that do qualify for inclusion. They are the Boyne curragh and the Donegal paddling curragh.

These two types of curragh and the seagoing curraghs do have one thing in common, however: it is the manner of their construction, which is essentially different from English and Welsh coracles, Spey curraghs, and Native American bull boats. As James Hornell explains, 'In British coracles the framework is put together mouth up, the bottom being the first part laid down. In Irish curraghs this procedure is reversed, the gunwale is formed first, the bottom and sides being put in position later, a procedure which results in the building of the curragh bottom upwards.'

THE BOYNE CURRAGH

'The lower reaches of the river Boyne, celebrated among archaeologists as the setting of one of the most remarkable groups of chamber tombs in Western Europe, have another claim on our interests as the last refuge of a venerable craft'. So wrote Estyn Evans, when referring to the Boyne curragh. This craft has all the characteristics of a British coracle. It is slightly ovate in shape, its paired hazel wands are regular and do not touch one another. It is propelled primarily by a single paddle, and is essentially an inland water craft. Boyne curraghs were being made and used in the traditional way (i.e. for the netting of salmon) until the 1 January 1948, when salmon netting above tidal waters was declared illegal.

They were used traditionally on the Boyne at Oldbridge, some four miles above Drogheda and, as has been mentioned already, near Slane castle. Hornell points out that 'in spite of the interest generally taken in this primitive species of craft, very little definite information is on record. The only important notice is that of W. F. Wakeman who made a drawing in 1848 of two of these curraghs at Strachallen, near Slane in County Meath. The mention of this place shows that the use of curraghs extended at that time considerably higher up the Boyne than at the present time'. (As Hornell carried out his two-year study in the early part of the twentieth century, presumably this the 'present time' to which he refers.)

The National Museum of Ireland has supplied me with photographs of two Boyne curraghs. One (Fig. 3:3) was registered in 1928. The other does not have a date, but looks to be of similar age. It did, however, emanate from the same approximate area as those seen by Wakeman, namely Slane.

Wakeman's description, as recorded by Hornell, is as follows :

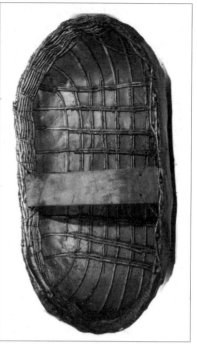

Fig 3 : 3
A Boyne curragh registered in the National Museum of Ireland, Dublin.

...a regular frame of willow ribs, generally laid in pairs, and extending along the sides and floor, formed the skeleton of the future boat, which was in the form of the bowl of a spoon, a little broader towards one end than the other, about 8 feet in length, but very nearly circular. The extremities of the ribs for a depth of about 18 inches from what would now be called the gunwale, were set in a very thick, strong and closely woven band of wickerwork, above which the ends of the rods slightly projected. Midships was thwart of ash, through which were rove thongs composed of twisted osiers, connecting the thwart or seat, with various portions of the abovementioned band, so as to bind the work together. The frame was then covered over the outside with a skin, untanned, of the horse or cow; and the result was the completion of a boat well adapted to the requirements of fisher men, and very useful, as I have experienced, as a means of crossing the Boyne at a place distant from any bridge or practicable ford.

This description fits either or both of the curraghs mentioned earlier, except for two things: firstly, the curraghs described are approximately 2' longer than the two shown in the photographs, and secondly, the accounts of curragh construction given by Hornell, Evans and, most importantly, O'Brien (see below) refer to the ribs being of hazel, and not willow as mentioned by Wakeman.

On 16 June 1930, one of the most renowned of all Boyne curragh-makers, Michael O'Brien of Oldbridge, County Meath, was interviewed on Ediphone record by John Delargy of Dublin. In this interview (later referred to as the 'Delargy interview') O'Brien laments that 'coracles' (the expression he used!) were dying out on the river Boyne of late. He went on to say:

> ...the last account I heard of coracle-makin' was at Lady
> Cunningham's of Slane castle. That's about twelve or fourteen years
> ago. And to the best o' my opinion it was a man of the name of
> Johnson that was making them there. He lived either in Slane or
> Rosnaree ... he was all his life at them ... I am about the last of the
> coracle-makers at Oldbridge at the present time.' His pessimism,
> however, proved to be ill-founded, because Evans records that
> Boyne curraghs were still being covered with hide, during a recent
> visit he made to the salmon fisheries near Drogheda.

He does not give a date for his visit but as he wrote his book in 1957, it is reasonable to assume it was well after 1930.

Hornell, referring to a widely-held belief in Ireland that the Boyne type of curragh was at one time in use on many rivers in Ireland, states: 'This hypothesis may be true, but the evidence for it at present is extremely scanty and applies almost entirely to streams within the confines of Ulster'. He cites anecdotal evidence of a round coracle having been used for net fishing on the Foyle in County Tyrone. But he also cites much more reliable eyewitness evidence relating to the survival of river curraghs on certain inland waters in the east of Ulster down to the end of the nineteenth century. For instance, he was told that in 1896-8 they were used for ferrying purposes between Omeath and Warren Point at the head of Carlingford Lough, and that they had survived on several streams in the Lough Neagh neighbourhood.

Once again, however, the perennial question arises: were they indigenous or 'borrowings' from the Boyne? In the 1980s I made extensive enquiries of the Ulster Folk Museum for evidence of coracle-like curraghs in the Province, but to no avail.

Boyne curragh construction

There is, happily, an abundance of written material on this subject. In the Delargy interview, for example, O'Brien describes how Boyne curraghs are made. Moreover, both Hornell and Evans have also provided full descriptions. Evans based his description on that set out by Hornell, which he regards highly, and amplified it as a result of his own personal observations. All three descriptions are fundamentally the same, although expressed differently. Hornell's relies strongly on a pictorial account which appeared in the *Illustrated London News*, dated 3 December, 1932.

During the last ten years, with the assistance of experienced basket-makers, I have had two replica Boyne curraghs made from the descriptions referred to above. No problems were encountered when following these instructions. One of these replicas is currently on display at the National Coracle Centre, Cenarth, west Wales.

Although there are no longer any traditional Boyne curragh-makers, left there are a number of people making excellent full-size replicas, both in the United Kingdom and in Ireland. Peter Faulkner, the Teme coracle-maker, is one such. His is not a true replica, because the seat on his craft is integrated into the gunwale of his craft and not slung on withy cords or ropes; also they do not have the system of braces running from the rear gunwale to the seat found in traditional-made Boyne curraghs, but otherwise they are very good likenesses.

Linda LeMieux, a Devon basket-maker, successfully uses self-made Boyne curraghs for reed-cutting. Olivia Elton Barratt uses the Boyne curragh as a basis for teaching people how to make rudimentary coracles on her courses.

In Northern Ireland, Bruce Crawford of Crawfordsburn, County Down, received a millennium award in May 1998 for a curragh project to develop and pass on the skills of Boyne curragh-making.

In the Republic of Ireland, the current Boyne curragh revival is led by Clive O'Gibne; Comhla Bheag, Donore and Meithal Mara, the well-known Naomhog makers, have an internet site which includes Boyne curraghs .

Fig 3 : 4
Boyne curragh and net.

Before passing from curragh construction, mention must be made of the Boyne curragh paddle. James Hornell describes the paddle thus: 'The paddle used is short, less than four feet in length. The blade is parallel-sided, flat on one surface, slightly curved transversely on the other'. In blade shape it is very similar to most Welsh and English paddles.

Boyne curragh usage
The principal use of the Boyne curragh was to catch salmon and, occasionally, trout by net. O'Brien in the Delargy interview mentions that the seasons from 1874 until 1884 were particularly prolific on the Boyne so far as salmon net-fishing was concerned . He states: 'I recollect one week we went down – me father used to have to go to Dublin market every morning, I might say, that time, with heavy loads o' fish – salmon an' trout ... we went down one Tuesday mornin' an' we took 27 salmon in one haul, an' the next morning we went down about an hour later an' we took 27 salmon in the same place ... An' that was the most remarkablest event I ever saw on the Boyne.'

Evans mentions an account of how Boyne curraghs were used. It is based on notes made at Oldbridge in 1947, and reads thus:

Every half-hour of daylight during the season, the curragh makes its brief trip with a draft net around the pool of water where the salmon lie below the weir. Its virtue lies in its lightness and ease of handling – though not for the novice – in the method of paddling over the bows, which allows it to keep close to the banks, and especially in the shallow draught which enables it to pass right under the weir without being swept down by the undercurrent. The paddler kneels in the deep bows and draws the boat along with rapid strokes alternately to left and right. The net man sits on the thwart facing backwards and pays out the net, the end of which is held by a third man on the bank. Having reached the far end of the weir the paddler races down stream and returns across the current to join the third man and close the net. The salmon are dispatched with a heavy 'priest', here called the killing stick…

O'Brien's account is substantially the same. What he does explain is that the net must be 'coiled proper' in the curragh. Fig. 3:4 illustrates how this is done.

Before leaving the Boyne curragh, reference must be made to a passage by James Hornell relating to this craft. He turns to a general consideration of curraghs, their origins and development, and states:

I consider in its boatlike forms, curragh design presents us with an instance of convergent evolution, where an old type, such as is represented in the Rosses curragh, has tended gradually to approach the plank boat type, rather than being originally a direct copy in wood, withy and hide of such a craft. It is, however, doubtful if the series thus reviewed is, in its entirety, a true evolutionary series. As will be seen later, certain considerations make it likely that the Boyne curragh is not a survival of a primitive first stage but represents a degradation of type, resulting the modification of a seagoing type such as that seen in the Rosses, to one suitable to the simpler needs of a salmon-fishing craft used on a gently flowing river.

I respectfully disagree, and suggest that the coracle (for that to all intents and purposes that is what the Boyne curragh is) and sea-going curraghs could have evolved quite separately. The requirement for a non-tidal or gently tidal river craft is quite different from that of a seagoing craft. Indeed, it is much more likely that mankind ventured onto inland rivers much earlier than he would have set forth on the sea. He would, moreover, have acquired the skills and tools to build a coracle much earlier than to construct a curragh. Indeed, one has only to look at a Native American bull boat to visualise what an early coracle would have looked like. It is submitted that the Boyne curragh is in every sense 'a survival of a primitive first stage'. It is suggested that the Donegal paddling curragh is an example of convergent evolution and it would, therefore, seem very appropriate to consider it now.

DONEGAL PADDLING CURRAGH
(*CURACH CEASSLA MA ROSSAN*)

Hornell heads his section the 'Curraghs of Donegal'; others refer to them as 'Rosses Paddling Curraghs', and one of their contemporary makers, 'Owey Island Curraghs'. Hornell's wider title is used but, in reality, it is those curraghs to be found in the Rosses district of the west coast of Ireland which will now be considered.

At first sight it might seem strange to include a seagoing curragh in a treatise dealing with coracles and allied craft. The reason for this is because it is in a sense the link between coracles and seagoing curraghs. Moreover, Donegal curraghs have significant features in common with coracles. For instance, they are not as elongated as seagoing curraghs. They are constructed in the same way as Boyne curraghs – they are carried by one person. But, above all, they are primarily paddled by a single paddler, albeit he is sometimes given assistance by the other member of the crew who sits in the stern.

Hornell justifiably refers to them as '... the crudest and most primitive type of seagoing curragh ...' He continues:

> ... eighty years ago this type was still in its rudest stage, the frame built up of withy ribs and stringers and covered with untanned hide. Today (i.e. the 1930s) the withy framework is replaced by a lattice frame of sawn and planed laths, while the cover, still retaining the original name of 'hide', is now made of two layers of tarred cloth. In Tory Island, side by side, with the survival of modified craft of this kind, are to be seen many wherein a close approximation has been made to the form and construction of a wood built dinghy. Taking the design as they were at the middle of the last century, together with those in use at the present, we have a perfect evolutionary gradation from a short and square one-man paddling type, without keel and thwarts, to an elongated boat-shaped design provided with permanent thwarts and rowed with oars pivoting on thole pins ...

Andrew McGonagle, a very experienced traditional Owey Island curragh maker, told me in 1993 that the thole pins, a removable thwart and a pair of oars were added to Donegal paddling curraghs about forty years ago 'as a standby in suitable conditions'.

Hornell confines the use of these curraghs to the Rosses district of the west coast of Donegal and the outlying islands, of which Tory Island is the most notable. McGonagle, having read what Hornell had to say on the subject, commented in a letter to me dated 13 July 1993 as follows: 'I have just read a book on currachs in Ireland by J. Hornell. Owey Island and its currachs are not mentioned yet Owey was the real home of the Donegal currach and its people were the acknowledged masters both of making and handling the currach. The places and the people mentioned would not be in the same class. So much for authentic history!'

In a slightly less hostile tone Estyn Evans states: 'I can add little to the historical account given by Hornell, but it should be noticed that the paddle curragh covered with horse hide was common in Erris, Co. Mayo, around 1830 and to judge from an entry in a Rathlin Island account book of 1760 – 'paid for one mare's hide for the boat 1s. and 6d – the paddle curragh was used there also'. The question must be asked: could the entry have related just as accurately to a Boyne curragh?

My sources of information relating to Donegal curraghs are Hornell, Estyn Evans, and Andy McGonagle.

I first met Andy McGonagle in 1992 when I was looking for paddling curraghs in the Rosses district of Ireland with members of Udaras na Gaeltachta. We had already come across a number of such craft. Finally we arrived at Andy's house in Kincasslagh, Co. Donegal. In due course he agreed to make me an Owey Island paddling curragh for the National Coracle Centre in west Wales. One year later I collected a superbly made craft which, Andy told me, was the first to have left Ireland (Plate 16). The handing-over and launching took place in the presence of the regional press and television service, together with a substantial number of members of the local community (Plate 17). The construction of this paddling curragh will be described later in this chapter.

Subsequently Andy told me many things, orally and in writing, about his curraghs and the people who used them. He came from an

Owey Island family with a long tradition of curragh manufacture and usage. He had been the island's postmaster until 1976, when he and the island's older men and women followed its younger men to the adjacent main land. He had used curraghs for at least forty-five years. Moreover, he recounted how his father and other Owey Island men made curraghs, and he had acquired his skills from watching and helping them rather than having been specifically taught. He went on to say that the curraghs had been used for fishing (particularly for Pollock), cutting seaweed, transporting animals to and from the mainland and shopping!, but that their current use was as inland ferries and for pleasure trips. Andy explained that the curraghs would travel some two to three miles into the open Atlantic, and were capable of coping with force eight conditions if they were encountered unexpectedly (Plate 18).

Interestingly he had been told that long before his time, curraghs on Owey were smaller, and that they were carried and paddled by women. He suggested that these craft may well have been coracles rather than curraghs. (It will be remembered that Native American women were the main users of bull boats, so his supposition should not be discounted.)

It is interesting to consider the McGonagle curragh. Of particular interest is the unusual lath formation in the extremity of the bow. It is typical of all Donegal paddling curraghs, but not to be found in any coracle-type craft, the nearest to it being the Dwyryd coracle from north Wales. (This coracle will be described in Chapter Four, which deals with the coracles of Wales.)

Donegal curragh paddling technique
In a letter dated 26 November 1992, McGonagle advised me as follows: 'Kneel upright at all times, do not sit down on the heels, and do not arch the spine or shoulders. Keep knees set apart and toes pressed against the toe support. Always keep the top hand on the 'fist' of the handle of the paddle. Do not allow any part of the body to come into contact with the frame of the currach while paddling.' He instructed me when we went to sea together in the curragh to use a 'scooping' motion on alternate sides of the bow. He said it was imperative to make the change of sides before the curragh started to move laterally with the paddle. This technique clearly differed

markedly from that used on coracles where the figure of eight or 'C' strokes were employed, with the position of the hands never changing.

Paddling curragh construction

'The shape in plan of these curraghs is that of a blunted ogive arch, with the sides nearly or quite parallel, apart from the bow region; the stern is truncate. The fore end is extremely bluff, rounding below very abruptly into the bottom which is transversely curved …'; so wrote Hornell:

> The modern practice is to construct the gunwale first, lay it on the ground with 'slots' cut to receive the oak laths which have been bent to shape. These are then wedged. The gunwale has a breastpiece to hold the two side pieces of the gunwale together. When this has been done, two thicknesses of material with a layer of brown paper between them are attached to the ribs and gunwale and 'tarred', traditionally with pitch and tar, but often nowadays with tar varnish. The outer hide generally is canvas or a similar material, but the inner is of a coarser cloth.
>
> Typical dimensions are as follows:
>
> Length overall: 8' 4" (504 cm); beam: 3' 7" (109 cm); depth: 1' 8" (51 cm), according to Meithal Mara, the curragh-makers referred to earlier.
>
> There are two types of paddle, an older and a newer; the older being more frequently preferred. McGonagle favours the former. It is usually made out of an old spade handle lashed or secured to a blade which is parallel-sided with long tapered shoulders. The blade is slightly curved backwards longitudinally. Its dimensions are as follows: overall length: 55"; loom: 25" long by 1½" diameter; blade: 23" long by 4½" wide; shoulders: 5-6" long; crutch: 4 by 1½". The newer type is marginally shorter, with its blade and loom being made of one piece of wood. Its dimensions are length: 52"; blade: 26 by 4½"; shoulders: 3" long; crutch: 4 by 1½.

Although Boyne and Spey curraghs vary in method of construction, their approximate size, weight and method of propulsion clearly bring them within the coracle category .

When the Spey Boyne and Donegal curraghs are considered together, a fundamental question arises: why, since the Donegal curragh still survives, and the Boyne curragh did so until after the end of the Second World War, has there not been a Scottish working curragh for over one hundred and fifty years? But now is probably not the appropriate time to attempt to give an answer, and it will be better done when all other coracles and allied craft have been considered, and conclusions drawn.

Chapter Four
WELSH CORACLES

Welsh coracles are particularly important for their rich diversity and variety of construction. M. Wight, writing about Welsh coracles in the 1960 autumn edition of *Country Quest*, states: 'A very interesting feature is the way in which the pattern of coracles differs on various rivers. This must be due in part to the nature of the streams, whether fast or slow, rocky or tidal, but it owes much to tradition, and until recently, never varied; even the form of the paddle is different on each river.'

Moreover, it is only in Wales that it is still possible to see net fishing practised in the traditional way.

Historical perspective
There is little doubt that skin-covered boats were used in Wales from pre Roman times. The writings of Caesar, Pliny and others make this clear. Moreover, 'corygeu' are named in *The Mabinogi*. It is very likely, however, that the craft referred to there were more akin to curraghs than coracles, which is not to say that coracles did not also exist at the same time. It is very likely that they did.

There are references to coracles in the dark ages. For instance, as already mentioned, a seventh-century lullaby contains the line 'Ef lledi bysc yng corwc' [*he kills fish in a coracle*], and, according to the laws of Hywel Dda, a coracle was worth eight pence. Moreover, James Motley, writing in *Tales of the Cymru* in 1845, states that 'a voyage in a covered coracle was one of the ceremonies of initiation into the mysteries of the ancient druids'.

The earliest clear description of a coracle in Wales is to be found in the account of Gerald Cambrensis in his journey through Wales with Archbishop Baldwin in 1188. He wrote 'for fishing and crossing rivers boats made of willow are used ... almost round in shape and covered with hides.' Having said this, nowhere does he indicate where in Wales he saw these coracles. It is very unlikely that he saw them on the Teifi, as he makes detailed reference to that area without making any specific reference to a coracle.

Two well-known 'Cywyddau' (Welsh poems in a special metre) give some idea of the shape and design of coracles in north east Wales. In one, Ifan Fychan ab Han ab Adda asks for a coracle from Sion Eutun, and in the second a reply is given by Maredydd ap Rhys, who lived between 1430 and 1450, on behalf of Sion Eutun. They are quoted at great length by J Geraint Jenkins, e.g. Cywydd 1: 'a bag of black skin preserves dry lathes' and 'it is shallow, made of a bull's tunic' and Cywydd 2: 'would the dark grey – black coracle take the fisherman to the pool.'

TEIFI CORACLES

The Teifi coracle (Plate 19) is probably the best known of all British coracles – although this assertion would be strongly challenged in Carmarthen! Coracles have been known on the Teifi from at least the last quarter of the eighteenth century. A witness to the Royal Commission of Inquiry into Salmon Fisheries in 1863 said: 'Coracle fishing has not been introduced on the Teifi from what I can gather above 60 years or something of that sort that is not to say they weren't used for transport and the like before then.'

Geraint Jenkins says that one time (1861) it was estimated that over three hundred coracles were being worked on the Teifi. Moreover, B. H. Malkin writing in *The Scenery, Antiquities and Biography of South Wales* (1804), states: 'There is scarcely a cottage in the neighbourhood of the Tivy ... without its coracle hanging by the door.'

In 1863 the Salmon Fisheries Acts were enacted, which led to the control of net-fishing by licensing as 'in fairness to the authorities, something had to be done to prevent serious over fishing'[1]. When the Reverend John Evans travelled the area in 1805 he noted that the supply of salmon far exceeded local demand and that a great deal of fish was dried, salted and 'exported'.[2]

Finally, by a bye-law confirmed by the Ministry of Agriculture and Fisheries on 14 February 1935, nets could only be used on the non-tidal stretches of the Teifi by a person who immediately before the coming into operation of the by-law was permitted to use a coracle in the water above Llechryd Bridge. As a result, net-fishing came to an end in 1970; the last licensed fisherman ceased to fish

Fig 4 : 1
Hannah Rees and Will Jones at Cenarth Falls. Date unknown.

through ill-health. So no longer is net-fishing permitted on the non-tidal waters of the Teifi, despite the fact that Cilgerran was once regarded as the Mecca of coracle net fishing. Abercych, another well-known fishing village on the Teifi suffered similarly.

Originally coracle net-fishing on the tidal sections of the Teifi took place at Llechryd and Cilgerran. For a few years, it also took place at Llandysul above Cenarth. but this came to an end when licensing was introduced on the Teifi.

Jenkins states that a witness who testified at the Inquiry in 1861 estimated that there were over three hundred coracles on the Teifi, and another thought that there were between two hundred and three hundred coracles at Cilgerran alone. At Cenarth there were only sixteen or eighteen nets, whilst Abercych had ten. He went on to say that in 1932 (before the restrictive bye-law was introduced) there were twenty-four coracles at Cenarth. Jenkins, writing in 1974, stated that then only five licensees were allowed to fish from coracles at Cilgerran.

This decline in net licences is dealt with in the *Report of the*

Committee on Salmon and Fresh Water Fisheries, 1964, at p.13. It reads: 'There is no doubt that interest in angling has vastly increased of recent years and that the increase is continuing; anglers contribute greatly to the tourist industry and the fishing tackle trade, some pay rates on sporting property to the local authorities in whose areas their waters lie and most contribute substantially to the funds of the river boards through licence duties. On the other hand commercial fishing ... employs comparatively few people and none of them is employed in the business all the time for there is a close season of at least 5 months; most of the fishing is done in public waters and there is therefore no contribution to local rates; and the amount of licence duty paid by the nets men is only in a few areas a noticeable contribution to the income of the river board.'

Thus it will be seen that the belief of the few remaining coracle net fishermen that they are not treated fairly by comparison with anglers can be well understood, particularly as they find recent increases of licence fees very hard to meet. Nowadays coracle net fishermen no longer work full-time on the Teifi, and of recent years have made little money out of their part-time activity.

The coracle visually

Many people over the years have attempted to describe what a Teifi coracle looks like (Plate 20), but none have bettered James Hornell's description, which is as follows:

> The Teifi coracle is short and of squat ungainly shape, in plan, broad and with very little horizontal curve at the fore end; nearly semi circular in plan at the after end. At the insertion of the seat, placed about mid length, the gunwale is pinched in at each side, giving the appearance of a slight waist between the forward and after sections. At the fore end and along the sides to a point just behind the seat, the coracle shows a slight degree of tumble-home, whereby the bottom view appears broader than the face plan and has no midships construction, its outline being bluntly triangular, with all the angles well rounded. The apex more rounded than the other angles, represents the stern. The gunwale sheers slightly towards the fore end, more emphatically towards the after end. The bottom is flat except for the last 12 – 15 inches, where it curves up gradually to the extremity of the stern.

It should be noted that:

1. The Teifi coracle is the only British coracle whose laths are of cleft willow. Indeed, the only other coracle to use willow in its construction is the Native American bull boat.
2. As there is only one transverse lath behind the seat, the structure is reinforced by a semi-circular plait of hazel withies (Plate 21). This ensures the flatness of its bottom, and is of crucial importance according to the two remaining traditional Teifi coracle-makers, Bernard Thomas of Llechryd and Ronald Davies of Cenarth, to whom I spoke at length in 2000 and 2001. No other coracle has a similar feature.
3. A comparison of coracles made at Cenarth and in Llechryd (Plate 22) reveals that whilst they are basically similar in design they differ slightly in shape; the stern of Thomas' coracle being noticeably more rounded than that of Davies. The writer has seen several coracles made by each man. They all have this same difference, which can only be explained as being due to contrasting traditions existing in Cenarth and Llechryd.

All Teifi coracles are now covered with calico. Davies has experimented with denim, and a well-known Cilgerran net fisherman, Roderic Bowen, who divides his time between Cilgerran and Boston, USA, uses a material which is made up of man-made and natural materials which he obtains in America.

Originally Teifi coracles were covered with hides like most other coracles but, in west Wales, flannel replaced animal hides. 'Flannel had replaced animal hides as a covering by the end of the Eighteenth Century and continued to be used until the mid Nineteenth Century': so states Jenkins. Moreover, J. R. Phillips, writing in 1867 in his *History of Cilgerran* (and quoted by Jenkins), said that flannel was used 'until recently for covering coracles at Cilgerran'. Additionally, Jenkins records that a Cilgerran fisherman, F. C. Llewelyn of Cenarth, said that his father used flannel until around 1880. There is no evidence of flannel having been used to cover coracles other than in west Wales.

Another innovation is to be found in the replacement of the traditional twisted hazel carrying-strap by the rubber tubing used to cover electrical cables: again, this is unique to the Teifi.

Finally, as on the river Tywi, a small number of coracles have been made of fibreglass. Some very experienced coracle-handlers, Bernard Thomas among them, prefer hazel and willow to fibreglass because they say they can 'feel' the river better in a craft made of natural materials.

What must be apparent from the above is that there have been a number of substantial constructional changes to Teifi coracles over the last two hundred-odd years.

Portage
The Teifi coracle is hoisted above the user's head with the carrying-strap being positioned across his upper chest. The 'claw' of the paddle is inserted into the basal bar beneath the seat, with the paddle resting on the right shoulder thus enabling the weight of the coracle to be better distributed. When a net is being used it is placed on the top of the coracle being carried.

Traditional coracle-makers
Bernard Thomas, the Llechryd coracle-maker, told the writer in 2001 that tradition dictated that there was only one coracle-maker in an area. Certainly this is the case today. He makes many coracles in Llechryd, but coracles in Cenarth are made by Ronnie Davies of that village. According to Ronnie, there now is a coracle-maker in Newcastle Emlyn whom he taught. Ronnie learnt his craft from the late J. C. Thomas, whom he succeeded as Cenarth coracle-maker. Ronnie made a coracle for me which became the starting exhibit in the 'Journey Zone' in the Millennium Dome in the year 2000. He is a very skilful and much respected coracle-maker (Plate 23).

Bernard Thomas, a sprightly octogenarian, is much better known further afield than Davies. To highlight the plight of net fishermen, he carried a coracle on his shoulders across London to the Houses of Parliament. He told me that he also paddled one to cause chaos at the boat race on the Thames for the same reason, and, most importantly, crossed the English channel in a Teifi coracle in the 1970s – the journey taking some fourteen hours.

Usage

The primary use of a Teifi coracle for very many years, and still today, is net-fishing. The method used is very similar to that used on the Tywi which will be dealt with in more detail later. So far as Teifi net fishing is concerned, the process can be described shortly. The hemp nets, made by the users, are strung out through horn rings and manipulated by horsehair ropes. The net is then towed downstream between two coracles, with the senior partner being in the left-hand side coracle. They paddle with one hand, handling the net rope with the other. When a fish is felt in the net, one man hauls rapidly on the rope causing the net to bunch up enclosing the fish. When the coracles have come together, the fish is removed and killed by a blow from the cnocer. The net is then spread across the river and they continue fishing until the end of their beat. They then return to the starting point and repeat the process ensuring that plenty of room is afforded to the pair coming next.

Rod and line fishing on the Teifi, although less frequent than net-fishing took place, as seen in a photograph of Hannah Rees, a noted local fisherwoman who reached the age of 100 (Fig. 4:1).

H. P. Wyndham, writing in *Tour through Monmouthshire and Wales* in 1774, describes how coracles were also used at Cilgerran for ferrying people across the river.

Bernard Thomas told me that Llechryd coraclemen regarded it as their duty to rescue sheep and cattle who had fallen into the river, or when it had burst its banks. So far as cattle were concerned the method used was to attach a rope to its mouth, not its horns, and tow it into midstream and allow it to swim against the current until it tired and then guide it to dry land.

After net-fishing, one of the best-known uses of coracles on the Teifi was in connection with 'sheep washing before clipping' (Plate 24).[3]

In Manordeifi church, on the banks of the Teifi, is to be found a coracle which was used in former times by the verger when the river flooded, which was a frequent occurrence. He used his coracle to rescue prayer and hymn books from the high-sided box pews. A coracle remains in the church today.

Coracle races and regattas

There is a strong tradition of coracle races on the Teifi but, inevitably, it is greatly reduced nowadays. Until quite recently there was a Boxing Day race from Llechryd bridge to Cardigan bridge, a distance of some twelve miles. Now the only regularly-held event is on a Saturday in Cilgerran, when a variety of races take place for cups every year. The standard of coracle-handling exhibited at this event is very high. The regatta is always very well supported by the local community. It is suggested that this is a strong indication of the virility of the coracle tradition on the river Teifi.

TYWI and COTHI CORACLES

'The Towey coracle is longer and with an elegance of form foreign to the short, squat Teifi type. The Teifi men do, however, pretend to despise the Towey design as departing from the ancient shape, and to some extent this is correct.' Thus writes James Hornell. He also refers to the use of sawn ash in place of cleft willow laths, a leather carrying-strap in place of one made of twisted hazel, and the absence of a plaited semi-circular reinforcing band such as is found in the stern compartment of a Teifi coracle. As distinguishing features this was undeniably true during the period between the wars, about which Hornell wrote, but events have moved on since then. Fibreglass is used, frequently but not exclusively, in the construction of Tywi coracles. In short, the distinguishing features of the Tywi coracle as mentioned by Hornell are merely progressive alterations of secondary importance. What is far more important is a consideration of the overall shape of the two types of coracle. It is submitted that when coracles are considered universally, and if it is accepted, as it must be, that the primary use of such craft was transportation, then it is apparent that the shape from which all coracles developed is circular. A consideration of the shapes of Native American bull boats and Iraqi quffas clearly establishes this premise. The shape of the Tywi coracle is much nearer this original shape than that of the Teifi coracle.

Historical

Jenkins' assertion that 'the history of coracle fishing on the Tywi as on other rivers of West Wales is obscure' would appear to be correct, but there is a clear body of evidence of usage from the eighteenth century onwards. Wyndham, writing in 1781, having described coracles he had seen on his tour continues: 'Riding through Abergwilly we saw several of these phenomena resting with their bottoms uppermost against the houses and resembling the shells of so many enormous turtles.'[4] (Modern Abergwili is some two miles east of Carmarthen on the Tywi.)

A wealth of historical material concerning the Tywi can be discovered when reading the transcript of a hearing before Sir William Jardine, Bart., W. J. Fennell Esq., and G. K. Richards Esq., on 27 September 1860 at Carmarthen, and held in the Museum of Welsh Life Archive.

For example, a witness was asked in what mode was fishing conducted on the Tywi. He replied, 'Coracle fishing is confined to the upper part of the river; when you get down near the seaside long drag nets are used.' Later on during his evidence he was asked about the condition of the fisheries in the vicinity of Carmarthen. He replied: 'I believe they manage to make a livelihood by fishing. I am told there are about 400 fishermen on the river from one end to the other.' When it was put to him that he thought there were four hundred fishermen representing nearly 2000 people living for seven months out of the twelve by salmon and sewin fishing on the Tywi, he replied: 'Yes – I think so'.

Another witness, who resided on the banks of the Cothi, an adjacent river to the Tywi, sung the praise of anglers. Having said that angling was much esteemed in the district, he went on: 'It has brought a good many strangers into the county.' The impression given was that very few locals were anglers, preferring to fish with nets.

A further witness, who was primarily concerned with the river Taf, made it clear that net fishing took place on the Cothi. This is the only direct evidence of the existence of net fishing on the Cothi, but its existence could be assumed from other comments made during the Inquiry.

Particularly revealing evidence was given by David Lewis, who worked his coracle between Carmarthen and Ferryside. He told the enquiry that the net used by coracles was a double one, explaining that: 'there is a big net before and a small mesh behind. The length of the net is about 20 yards, and I should think this would take a 1 lb fish.' He went on to say that they only fished towards the sea. He stated that the period for fishing on the Tywi was from April until about August for sewin, adding: 'In August, we put the sewin nets away, and use nets for salmon only.' He was asked if the small-meshed nets were generally used by the fishermen who have coracles, to which he replied: 'By everyone; no other net is used'. He was further asked where he sent his fish for sale, to which he replied: 'Sometimes we sell it in the town, and at other times send it away'. He was then asked how many people live solely by salmon and sewin fishing, to which he replied about two hundred who had no other employment.

Finally, he referred to the practice of the coracle net fishermen known as 'bush fishing'. He described how 'some of the coracle fishermen above Carmarthen used to catch the spawning sewin. The sewin spawn under bushes generally, and they set some nets around the bushes to take sewin when they are spawning.'

Finally, Geraint Jenkins draws attention to the fact that 'although many Carmarthen coraclemen like Raymond Rees (about whom more later) are not Welsh-speaking, their terminology and fishing nomenclature is always in the Welsh language, and the persistence of fishing terms, probably from medieval Welsh, may be an indication of the antiquity of the coracle and the coracle net.' He gives a number of examples of such words as are in use on both the Teifi and the Tywi. This was confirmed by Raymond Rees when I spoke to him about it in 2001 at his home in Carmarthen.

The coracle community

Raymond Rees very generously made available to me extracts from the occurrence book in use at Carmarthen police station during the nineteenth century. It is apparent when reading these police reports that a high level of drunkenness, extreme abuse and fighting was rife, which involved to a large extent the Carmarthen fishermen and their wives.

Byron Rogers, a Carmarthen man, described a conversation he had some years ago with William Elias, a former coracleman who described the coraclemen of his youth thus: 'They had this siege mentality, it was them against the world, not that they had much idea about the world. Theirs was about one mile on the river Towy ... They were known as the Red Light Boys' on account of the red lights on the railway bridge they passed under ... They were as hard as nails ... after the booze and fags nothing could carry them off except old age'. This article ironically appeared in a *Saga* magazine.

From an account of a case of poaching using coracles, before the Carmarthen Petty Sessions on 29 January 1859, it is apparent that poaching, during the close fishing season, was far from unknown.

The skill exhibited in coracle-handling from a very early age is graphically illustrated in an account which appeared in the *Carmarthen Journal* of 15 August 1913. Sidney Elias (a very common surname amongst Carmarthen coraclemen) was presented with a framed certificate for gallant conduct. The account reads: 'On 13 June 1913 [at] the Quay, Willie Phillips accidentally fell into the Towy near the Mission church when the river was in full flood, and Sidney Elias, seeing the imminent danger in which his friend was situated, displaying great presence of mind in one so young jumped into a coracle, and paddling the frail craft a short distance, promptly threw a rope into the river for Phillips to seize, and safely hauled the latter, thereby effecting a very plucky rescue.' This incident not only illustrates the skill in handling a coracle by a young man, but also the abundance of such craft which enabled young Elias to effect his rescue.

Uses

The most important contemporary use of a Tywi coracle, is undoubtedly net fishing.

I am greatly indebted to Raymond Rees, the noted Carmarthen coracle-maker and net fisherman for the following description given to me in 2001. He described that when fishing, two coracles are used, a net being towed downstream between them on the ebb tide. This net consists of two sheets of netting fixed together in such a way as to form a bag as they are towed through the water. The net is suspended from a head rope which contains cork floats at evenly spaced intervals along its length and a foot rope which is weighted to keep the net on the bed of the river. A free-running line is threaded through the corks and made fast at one end, whilst hand lines are fixed to both ends. In operation, the more experienced coracleman holds the free-running line as well as a hand line, his partner holding the other line loosely, and when a fish is felt the free-running line is pulled, causing the net to bunch trapping the fish in the bag. He went on to explain how the head and foot ropes, hand lines and free-running lines were home-spun from the tail hair of a cow.

The net, however, has undergone changes with the advent of new materials such as nylon, polythene, polypropylene etc. Whilst it is still handmade, nowadays man-made fibres are used. The complete net is about 33 feet long, 2 feet deep and weighs between 3 and 4 lbs. It is a single-walled trammel net. Rees explained that successful fishing very much depends on the accurate setting and weighting of the net and, of course, the skill of the coracleman controlling it. After very many years experience Rees has perfected a mathematical formula which greatly simplifies problems encountered when weighting and setting the net.

Fishing on the Tywi is carried out by night, the beginning of the session being at twilight: 'as soon as seven stars appear in the sky fishing can begin'. Jenkins states:

> ... and it always begins nearer the right bank of the river. The area fished is from the Pump House near the old Carmarthen Railway Station to near the estuary. It comprises a large number of pools. The first pair of coracles on the river bank with a net in place inside one of them is the first to begin the trawl. It is important that the net be inside the coracle or the pair will forfeit their turn. After the first pair have drifted with the ebb tide 'to meet the fish' that swim up stream, for about 200 yards or in line with a pre determined mark on the river bank such as a certain tree or rock, one of the coraclemen beats his cnocer against the side of his craft. This is the signal for the 2nd pair of coracles in the queue on the river bank to enter the water.

The coracle itself
Of all the British coracles the Tywi coracle has changed the most. In essence there are now three different types of Tywi coracle; the differences are of construction, not of overall shape.
The original (Fig. 4:2) was made of sawn ash laths with a woven gunwale of hazel. The laths consisted of an equal number of longitudinal and transverse laths, namely seven, together with two

interlacing diagonal laths and four interwoven laths with the first four transverse laths. These laths do not extend up the sides. The seat is supported by a solid bulkhead (Plate 25).

The covering of a Tywi coracle provides an excellent illustration of the historical development of the coracle. Wyndham, writing in 1781, refers to a coracle being 'covered with raw hide or strong canvas'. Wight, however, states that 'with the rise of the Welsh woollen industry in the sixteenth century came the use of thick flannel in place of hides for covering coracles. In 1798 the overseer at Llanegwad on the Towy was ordered to supply flannel and other materials for making a coracle for a poor man, so that he can earn a living

Fig 4 : 2
Raymond Rees carrying a traditional Tywi coracle.

with it.' He also pinpoints 1870 as the year in which Henry Evans of Carmarthen experimented with calico.

The original Tywi coracle, as well as a paddle, which was unusually long, carried a cnocer for killing fish, and a bailer (the only coracle to do so). This was because Tywi coracles operated in broad tidal waters, often rough and broken.

Raymond Rees explained that because the gunwale of the original coracle consisted of woven hazel, which called for considerable basket making skills to construct, not widely possessed in recent times, the practice was adopted of substituting a laminated gunwale made of sawn ash lengths. This change gave rise to the second type of Tywi coracle. Apart from the gunwale it does not differ from the traditional craft. Both types of coracle exist today, but it is the second type which is in greater numbers than the original.

Finally, in the early 1970s the most recent development in the manufacture of Tywi coracles occurred. Fibreglass became widely used, to counteract bumping on the bottom of parts of the river with a greatly reduced water level. The advantages of fibre glass is that it is light, durable and is easily maintained. It is the third type of Tywi coracle (Plate 26).

Before the use of fibreglass was pioneered, attempts were made, Raymond Rees said, to improve further the fishing coracle by using materials which were more easily maintained and longer-lasting than those of the traditional coracle. This was in the 1940s, when aluminium was experimented with, as it was widely available at the time. It was light, strong and rust-proof, but, Raymond said it was 'easily dented and considered too inflexible.' As a result, only one was ever made. It will be seen later in this chapter that aluminium was used in coracle construction at Llangollen on the Dee.

Licensing
Although as recently as the 1920s there was not any limitation on the number of coracles fishing on the Tywi, the total number of coracles in use did not exceed forty-eight pairs. However, by the end of the decade the number of licenses issued had reduced to twenty-five, and by 1939 only twelve licenses were issued. This number has remained static until the present day, according to Raymond Rees. Hornell, writing about the pre-war period, states: 'The Ministry of Agriculture and Fisheries has sought to abolish this method of fishing [coracle net fishing] in the interests of fishery conservation' – a sentiment echoed earlier, it will be recalled, in relation to attitudes taken by those in authority to Teifi coracle net fishing.

Throughout the 1990s the Carmarthen Coracle Netsmen's Association fought a persistent battle with the authorities who have sought to diminish the rights of their members. Examples are cutting the fishing season by a month, and recently banning men from taking their sons on the water to teach them the requisite skills – this was reported in the *Daily Telegraph* of 11 March 1996. Also licence fees have been very substantially increased.

Personalities

Every river has its personalities amongst its coraclemen past and present; the Tywi is no exception. So this probably the best way to end a consideration of the coracle on the Tywi and those associated with them. Most notable are a grandfather and his grandson, both already mentioned, William Elias BEM and Raymond Rees.

William Elias (Fig. 4:3) is unique in being the only

Fig 4 : 3
William Elias BEM of Carmarthen
(grandfather of Raymond Rees)

man to be honoured by the Monarch for 'services to coracle fishing'. He fished until he was over 85, and in doing so was following the tradition of his grandfather and great-grandfather before him. He left school early, explaining to Byron Rogers, 'I suppose I should have stuck more to school, but once you get on the river there's no going back. It gets into your blood.'

Raymond Rees (see Fig. 4:2) is the maternal grandson of William. He did remain at school and ultimately became a civil servant, but also from an early age both made and used all three types of Tywi coracle. There is no-one living who knows more about the Tywi coracle and net fishing than Raymond Rees. He has his own very informative website and, in addition to his practical skills as a coracle-maker and user he is a keen student of everything to do with the coracling way of life. Indeed he was so well-regarded by Dr J. Geraint Jenkins that he asked Raymond to provide the foreword to his book, *The Coracle*. Latterly Raymond has ceased to work as a civil servant and, until recently, ran his own fishmonger's shop in Carmarthen market, selling, amongst other fish, those taken by coracles.

Finally, the name of Michael Elias, in his role as secretary of the Carmarthen Netsmen's Association, appears very frequently in the national as well as local press championing the cause of the Tywi coraclemen against the river authorities. He comes from a family with a three hundred year-old tradition of coracle net fishing, and still fishes from his coracle today as well as working full-time.

TAF CORACLES

Consideration is now given to the only other river on which net fishing with coracles is permitted under licence, namely the river Taf, which is based at the village of St Clears, some eight miles from Carmarthen. (It is not to be confused with the river Taff at Merthyr Vale, some considerable distance away.) It is a short river, about thirty-two miles long, that runs into the sea in Carmarthen Bay. It shares a common estuary with the Tywi.

The Taf is unique in that it has the only ghost associated with coracles. Hornell, quoting from the *South Wales Evening Post*, 20 June 1935, describes how 'Admiral Laugharne, a noted character in former times, is said to appear naked furiously ferrying himself across the stream in a coracle, bailing it out the while with a cocked hat.'

Historical

In 1805, Donovan E, in his *Descriptive Excursions through South Wales & Monmouthshire*, describes seeing at St. Clears 'a number of poor inhabitants of the neighbouring cottages eagerly pursuing their customary occupations in the coracle fishery'. He was particularly impressed with the skill shown in coracle-handling on the Taf. Somewhat later, in 1860, a witness, Captain Rhys Pryse Beynon, giving evidence to the Commission already mentioned, stated that he lived within two miles of the banks of the Taf. He went on to confirm that there was a sewin fishery on the Taf. He was asked how the fish were taken and replied: 'By nets and coracles, in the same way as you have heard described on the Tywi. All sorts of mesh were used.' Later he replied, in response to a question by the Commission, 'I have fished a great deal in coracles with sweep nets and all other nets.'

Another witness, John Beynon, was asked how many boats were employed in taking salmon on the Taf, to which he replied: 'Between 40 and 50.' He went on to say that 'they are considerably less than they were 20 years ago.'

From the above it will be seen that coracle net fishing thrived on the Taf in the nineteenth century, a very different situation from that which prevails today, as will be seen later.

Licensing

A limitation order was introduced in 1931 which permitted coracle net fishing to be carried out only under license. The decline in net fishing is graphically shown by considering what Hornell said, when writing about the inter-war period: 'Net fishing is still permitted, 3 licenses being in force in 1935, but they are to be reduced, to two in the near future.'

This is slightly at variance with what Jenkins, writing in 1974, said: 'The number of coracles on the Taf has remained constant since 1935, 2 pairs being licensed at that time. In 1933, 3 coracle nets were licensed.' He went on to record his deep concern at attempts made, he believed, during an inquiry where it was proposed to change the boundary of coracle net fishing in 1971 which, if it had succeeded would have been 'tantamount to total prohibition of net fishing on the river Taf.' There remains only one license to fish on the Taf, it was held by the late Edgworth Evans (about whom more later) who sadly died during 2001. It is now held by another.

The coracle itself

Like the situation on the Tywi, the Taf coracle has undergone considerable change. Both Hornell and Jenkins assert that in size and shape there is a strong resemblance with the Tywi coracle, but because a wattled gunwale such as was found in the Carmarthen craft calls for the skills of the basket-maker, it has been replaced by one made of planking, which makes for much easier constructional skills.

A comparison between the traditional Taf coracle in Fig. 4:4 and a modern one attributed to the late Edgworth Evans (Fig. 4:5)

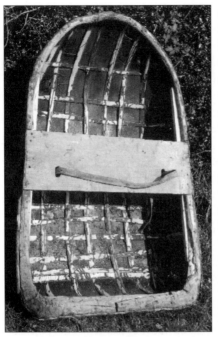

Fig 4 : 4
A traditional Taf coracle believed to have been made by Irlwyn John.

demonstrates the variation in Taf coracle construction. It is submitted that whilst the Evans craft resembles a Tywi coracle, the traditional Taf coracle more closely resembles a Teifi coracle.

Hornell describes a typical Taf coracle of the inter-war years thus:

The lattice part of the framework consists of 7 longitudinal frames interlaced with either 5 or 6 transverse ones, all made of rough laths, 1¼-1½ inches wide. No diagonal laths are present but 2 or 3 accessory laths, to strengthen the bottom under the feet, may be intercalated with several of the foremost transverse frames. The ends of all the frames, bent up in the usual manner, are inserted, after being whittled to cylindrical points about 3/8 inches in diameter, into vertical holes made at intervals in a broad gunwale frame of thin board. The seat is set flush with this gunwale, cleats below joining it to the gunwale frame which does not extend beneath the seat. The partition supporting the after border of the seat is made of a number of broad strips of thin board set vertically at short intervals apart. They are nailed below to a basal bar extending across the bottom, while above they are nailed to a long cleat screwed to the underside of the seat. The cover is of calico, coated with a mixture made by boiling pitch with Stockholm tar. A round drainage hole is cut in the cover at the tail end, high up, for the easy emptying of water when the coracle is taken out of the water.

He describes the paddle as being of a similar length to that used on the Tywi.

Finally, he states that a cnocer is carried in the pocket as being handier than when kept in a loop on the seat. One of the unusual features of this type of Taf coracle is the method of insertion of the laths into the gunwale which is not to be found in Welsh, Scottish and English coracles, but is encountered in early Irish curraghs. Another unusual feature is

Fig 4 : 5
Modern Taf coracle made by Edgworth Evans.
Date Unknown.

hinted at by Hornell but clearly described by Jenkins, when he recounts being told by Raymond Rees (who knew the Taf and its coraclemen intimately) that 'to build a Taf coracle of the older variety a naturally curving branch of a tree, usually an apple tree, was cut and split in half to form the fore part of the gunwale. The 2 sections were fixed together with a cleat iron. Another branch was treated in the same way to form the rear gunwale'.

The modern Taf coracle, referred to earlier, has a gunwale which was constructed in exactly the same way as the gunwale of a modern Tywi coracle. The craft is longer and narrower than the traditional coracle and it had two long diagonal laths running the full length of the craft. Finally, the cnocer was carried in a loop secured to the thwart. These variations may well be due to the fact that Evans was the sole license holder and had a very close working and personal relationship with the Tywi nets-men in general, and Rees in particular. This view is reinforced by the fact that by the 1980s Evans was using a fibreglass Taf coracle.

Personalities
The late Edgworth Evans of St Clears (Plate 27) shared

Fig 4 : 6
Irlwyn John, traditional Taf coracle-maker

demonstrations of coracle-making and handling skills with Raymond Rees, of Carmarthen. Evans died, much lamented, in 2001. He had been on the Taf since he was ten, and was a jealous protector of the river and the fish which swam in it.

A debt of gratitude is owed to Alan and Nina Grove of Kidderminster who interviewed Irlwyn John (Fig. 4:6), a retired 80-year-old Taf net fisherman, who had made a traditional Taf coracle for the Museum of Welsh life in 1940, and later gave it to them in 1988.

Irlwyn John was born in St. Clears. His earliest memories are of his father and a neighbour, David Walters, net fishing with coracles on the Taf in the 1930s. In those days net fishing was permitted from underneath Woolstone down to Bridgend bridge, but now it is confined from Bridgend bridge to lower St. Clears. He went on to relate that his father and grandfather (Benjamin John) not only used but also made coracles. He named other St. Clears men who fished with nets and coracles in addition to his father, grandfather and David Walters. They were Howell and Willy Walters, Benjamin and Jack Davies, the late Edgeworth Evans, Huw Evans and Dewi Williams. He knew of Billy Beynon, whose photograph appears at page 164 of Jenkins book *Nets and Coracles*.

Irlwyn made some illuminating comments concerning the making of traditional Taf coracles. He was asked why an apple tree was used for the gunwale. He replied that it was the way in which apple trees bend and that their curves, which are needed, could be seen. He explained that it was extremely difficult to find the right piece, which had to be long enough to reach the seat. When found it was split into two halves to form the bow section of the gunwale. It was suggested that Taf coracles had such gunwales to avoid having to weave a gunwale such as was found on Teifi or Tywi coracles. He refuted the suggestion, saying, 'No – that's not true – you see it was all about the river. The stretch of the Taf we fished was very narrow and the banks steep, we were continually bumping the sides and the apple wood frame withstood the knocks better … apple wood doesn't split when nailed or pegged and is very durable.' He explained that the stern gunwale was made of hazel or willow, whichever was to hand, as long as it bent well.

He described how this section of the gunwale was bent, saying, 'Well, the way we did it, down on the farm (there was always plenty of wood, you see) was to build a big fire and cover it with grass cuttings and the rod for the back of the gunwale was placed over the fire. The heat and the steam softened the wood so that we could bent it round a barrel and it took many of us to do it. We then left it for several weeks tied to the barrel to dry and set to shape.

He went on to deal with the catching of salmon and sewin by nets and coracles, explaining that an average nightly catch was about 30-40 pounds.

CLEDDAU and NEVERN CORACLES

Pembrokeshire has two rivers on which coracles were used, but no longer. They are the Cleddau and the Nevern.

Cleddau coracles

Hornell states that 'a single pair of coracles are all that remain on the eastern branch of this river; none is to be found on the western. The pair on the eastern branch belong to Mr. G. W. Pike, Blackpool Flour Mills, near Narberth.' (It will be remembered that he was writing about the situation which pertained between the Wars.) By the time Jenkins wrote *Nets and Coracles* (published in 1974) there were no longer any coracles left on either branch of the Cleddau.

According to Jenkins, even in the 1860s there were never more than six pairs above Llawhaden bridge and six to ten below. A witness to the Inquiry mentioned earlier, S. Harford-Landowne (p.122) confirmed that coracle fishing was practised 'mostly from the weir at or about Llawhaden down to Blackpool.' By 1930, Jenkins reported, there were only three pairs, reducing to a single pair by 1934, coracle fishing having come to an end by the early 1940s.

Whilst there are photographs of traditional Cleddau coracles in existence (Fig. 4:7), no craft remain. Interestingly, however, Mr W. G. Pike of Kilgetty in July 1977 provided 'Directions for the Construction of the Coracles as used on the Eastern Cleddau River up to 1937' to the Welsh Folk Museum, as it then was. From these, a replica Cleddau coracle was built, which is in the Museum of Welsh Life.

The coracle itself

The Cleddau coracle's laths are 1½ inches wide, and made of sawn ash. The gunwale is made of wood 1½ inches square. The bow is much straighter than that of a Teifi coracle, which it most closely resembles. It has six longitudinal laths, six transverse in front of the seat and two behind it.

Unusual features of this coracle are:

1. It is covered with hessian canvas, made waterproof with a mixture of Swedish pitch and Stockholm tar, and ...

Fig 4 : 7
A traditional Cleddau coracle c. 1936.

2.   ... it has an unusual shaped paddle. Hornell states that the paddle
     has a loom ending in a transverse claw grip, identical to that of a
     Teifi paddle. However, the loom of the Teifi paddle is topped
     with a claw grip, but it is in the same plane as its loom, not
     transverse to it as in the case of the Cleddau. The Cleddau
     coracle measured by Hornell had a length of 52 inches, a width of
     40 inches, and a depth of 14 inches.

Poaching

Jenkins states 'that the coracles were used frequently for poaching'. This is borne out by an incident recorded in *The Story of Blackpool Mill* by Sir Francis Dashwood, Bt., a monograph about the Mill situated on the banks of the Cleddau and tenanted in the past by the Pike family. At page 4, he wrote: 'The Mill leat was a favourite place for catching fish and people used to fill their baskets with little salmon known as 'shed'. Near the weir there was a fish trap known as 'the Slaughter', and as many as 40 or 50 sewin were caught at a time there.'

Not unnaturally, this abundance of fish encouraged poaching, which was carried out extensively, but matters came to a head in 1830 when there was a violent clash at Blackpool between the poachers and the men of Baron de Rutzen. The Baron had previously taken to court two Llewellyns [sic] who questioned the right of the Baroness to the fishing. The Magistrates let them off with a warning against any further poaching.

Some time later the Baron was warned that poachers were planning to net the river on a certain night. So his agent, Wm Currie, collected twenty men and they watched the river. In due course John and Isaac Llewellyn were spotted coming downstream, each in a coracle, and netting the draw pool between Blackpool and the weir. Currie asked them to stop several times but they refused to take any notice. So two of Currie's men seized the coracles and pulled them ashore. One of the Llewellyns shouted 'murder', and immediately squibs were fired from the lime kiln and horns were sounded in the wood.

As the coracles were being carried to the bridge, a large party of men, some armed with sticks, set upon Currie's men. In the ensuing fight six of Currie's men were beaten and two seriously injured. Currie himself only just escaped, pursued by several men. The Llewellyns were subsequently taken to court, where they pleaded guilty on the understanding that they would not be indicted providing the offence was not repeated.

Nevern Coracles

The Nevern is a short stream, some thirteen miles long, running from the Preseli Hills to the sea at Newport, Pembrokeshire. It flows into Newport Bay, south of the Teifi and north of the Tywi.

According to Jenkins, Nevern coracles were similar to Teifi coracles, and even in the 1860s no more than four pairs of coracles operated above the tideway. Confirmation of the existence of coraclemen can be found in the evidence of John Harris, a local man and Receiver of Wrecks, who was asked by the Commissioners in 1861 whether there were any coracles employed above the tideway. He replied in the affirmative, but added that he did not think there were more than four coracles on the Nevern. Discord between the coracle netsmen and the Seine netsmen of the estuary was constant. It is well summed up in an extract from the minutes of evidence taken before the Commissioners appointed to enquire into salmon fisheries (England and Wales) in 1861, at page 136. It reads: 'The men that fish the sand and those who fish the river are quite different men; the coracles belong to the men who fish the river and they are the men who give most trouble, the men at the mouth are fair fisher men.'

CORACLES ON THE TAFF

The river Taff (not to be confused with the already mentioned west Wales river Taf) runs through Cardiff. It was well known for a drowning incident in 1908 involving a three-year-old boy, Cromwell Davies. Gareth Thomas, in the December 1998 edition of *Picture Postcard Monthly*, displayed a copy of a postcard he had discovered entitled: 'Little Cromwell Davies found in the Taff at Quaker's Yard'. It shows five men standing in the shallows of a river (which is clearly the Taff). Three coracles lie at the waters edge. One of the men has a coracle on his back and is holding a paddle and a length of rope.

Thomas researched the incident in considerable detail. From what he established, it became clear that coracles played a significant part in the search for the child. There is little doubt that the five men and four coracles shown in the postcard were involved. There is absolutely no doubt that the coracles were Tywi coracles and the men from Carmarthen. This led people to believe that in 1908 local coraclemen did not exist, otherwise they would have participated in the search for the little boy, and accordingly there was not any coracle tradition on the Taff. However, a search of the local records at Cardiff revealed that a family of coraclemen existed who fished on the Taff where the Royal Hotel was later built. Moreover, in Cardiff Records, volume 5, Chapter 6, under the heading 'Reminiscences of old inhabitants', one William Lucas Evans stated, 'I remember coracles being used at Cardiff as long as I can remember anything' (he was 84 at the time he said this). He went on to say old Mr James Lucas, the fisherman, was drowned about seventy years ago (circa 1825) in endeavouring to get to the land opposite the Blackfriars from his coracle, during an immense flood of the Taff such as often occurred before the river was straightened. 'He was of an old Cardiff family of fishermen ... 40 years or more ago (circa 1854) Mr J. Lucas could be seen drawing salmon from his coracle at the site of the present Royal Hotel'.

Furthermore, J. C. Ibbetson (1759-1817), the well-known artist, produced a painting entitled *Cardiff from the West*. It depicts one coracle afloat and two being carried on the foreshore of the same river, which clearly is the Taff. The coracles in the painting are very large, vaguely like a Teifi coracle in shape, but much squarer. The paddles are Tywi-like in length and overall appearance. The coraclemen also carried a long pole, which was no doubt used for stimulating movement by salmon or sewin. Interestingly, Donovan E, writing of Cardiff in the first decade of the nineteenth century, 'was impressed with the quantity of sea trout taken from the river Taff where he observed fisherman taking them in vast quantities in their nets.'

It must be observed that no mention of coracles was made, nor is it clear whereabouts on the Taff, Donovan saw what he did. If it were upriver, it is reasonable to expect coracles to have been used, but if it were nearer the river's mouth, other forms of netting would more likely to have been employed. In summary, therefore, whether coracles were in use locally or not at the time of the Cromwell Davies incident in 1908, it is clear that they were used for fishing with coracles on the Taff in earlier times.

LOUGHOR (*LLWCHWR*) CORACLES

Jenkins writes that 'bowl-shaped nearly square coracles were used on the river Loughor at Pontardulais during the nineteenth century'. Moreover, Donovan states: 'half a dozen females seated upon the

Fig 4 : 8
Worshippers crossing the river Llwchwr in their coracles from the Hendy
side to a service at the Old Church.

panniers of their ponies ... rode hastily down to the market place with a supply of sewin conveyed from Pontardulais, about ten miles to the westward abounding with fish during the summer, being caught in the coracle fisheries by the peasantry'. He was writing primarily about Swansea market.

In the archives of the Museum of Welsh Life (MS 650/1) there is correspondence between J. Herbert W. Edmund and T. H. Thomas of Cardiff. In a letter from Pontardulais dated 30 September 1891, Edmund makes mention of the presence of coracles on the Loughor, stating: 'they are devoid of the wicker adornment 'though the older fisher men recall the time when it was not considered the thing to use a coracle without such evidence of the maker's skill ... they were in use on the river 12 coracles through out the late season ending 31st August'.

In another letter between the same parties, Edmunds makes further reference to Loughor coracles comparing their overall shape with that of a Teifi coracle. A photograph (Fig. 4:8) contained in the Pontardulais Picture Archive confirms Edmunds' account.

CORACLES on the river WYE (in Wales), and NEARBY RIVERS AND LAKES

Coracles were also to be found on the south eastern rivers of Wales, namely the Wye, Usk and Monnow. Reference has already been made to these coracles under the section on English coracles, but their manufacture and use was not confined to the English Wye. They were also made and used where the river flowed through Wales. Their construction and manner of use is as in Chapter Two, but although the Welsh Wye coracle is basically the same as the English Wye version, the nearby rivers Usk, Monnow and Lugg are exclusively Welsh and merit individual attention.

USK

Construction
When the photograph of Tom Rees, one of the last coracle users (Fig. 4:9) is compared with the Wye coracle currently in the Hereford museum, it will be seen that they are identical in construction, as is rightly claimed by Hornell and Jenkins.

History
The earliest mention of coracle usage in the Usk area is to be found in Camden's *Britannia*. It relates to the year 1586. He records that 'two miles to the east of Brecknock, is a large lake which the Britons call Llyn Savaddan ... in English 'tis called Brecknock Mere; it is two miles long and the same breadth, well stocked with otters and also perches, tenches and eels which the fishermen take in the coracles'. (He was referring to Llangors Lake.) The author of *Usk Past and Present,* written in about 1892, confirms that Usk coracles were used for both netting and angling. He concludes by saying 'on the banks of the Usk ... these coracles were to be seen hanging at the doors of many of these cottages'. Usk coracles were used for angling as well as net fishing. Net fishing ended by the First World War but angling continued until Thomas Rees died in 1933.

Hanbury Tennison archive
In 1996-7 correspondence took place between Sir Richard Hanbury

Fig 4 : 9
Thomas Rees, last coracle fisherman on the Usk, and his Usk coracle.

Tennison and me. In a letter dated 17 January 1997, Sir Richard referred to the Crown Fishery which extended from a point five miles up river from the town of Usk to a point downstream not far from Caerleon. The fishery had been in his family's possession from about 1759 until 1924. He stated that prior to 1860 salmon fishing was always let to professional net fishermen, 'some of whom will have used coracles.' He continued, 'after 1860 the fishing was let to, and administered by the United Usk Fishery Association whose second Chairman was one Arthur Berrington (who will be referred to later). Apparently at various times during Sir Richard's family's tenure of the Crown Fishery, attempts were made to prevent the estate's tenants from fishing or to establish rival fisheries. This inevitably led to litigation, particularly when in 1766 a fishing tenant, Phillip Reece, was sued for causing damage to adjoining farmlands. Amongst other things he was accused of was 'hauling diverse fishing nets'. Reece apparently pleaded 'ancient rights'.

Sir Richard, deriving his knowledge from the estate records, relates that several witnesses testified during a court hearing. Examples he cited were as follows: 'William Howell stated the method of fishing was with coracles, one at each end of the net. William Jenkins, then aged 70, also testified that he and his father, one James Morris, used to fish with coracles and landed the coracles and nets at Inys y Bont'. Finally, James Glow gave evidence that 'he had often seen men leave their coracles and dry their nets on an apple tree while they went to drink ale'.

Further, the estate records showed that in 1797 Sir Samuel Fludyear, Bart., who owned the salmon weir at Trostey, claimed a right to fish with a small net and two coracles. From the same source it appeared that the Duke of Beaufort claimed a right to fish at Monkswood (Usk) with two men and either a small net worked with coracles or a larger net worked with boats. Finally, in May 1901 the earlier-mentioned Arthur Berrington replied to a question from a judge in another law suit: 'Q. There is another mode of fishing on the river called coracle fishing? A. That used to be used. There is none now but it used to be used in my time.' (Arthur Berrington had previously testified that he had fished the Usk since 1847.)

This correspondence was prompted by a letter written to The Times by Sir Richard Hanbury Tennison in which he had stated that a 68½ pound salmon had been taken in a net trawled by a coracle on the Usk in 1782!

Monnow and Lugg Coracles
James Hornell, writing in the 1940s, states: 'on the rivers Usk and Wye and on their main tributaries of which the Monnow and Lugg are the most important, coracles were regularly employed by fishermen until a few decades ago.'

CORACLES ON THE RIVER DYFI

On the west side of Wales in the Machynlleth area is to be found the river Dyfi.

Coracles have not been used on the Dyfi for very many years. The earliest reference to coracle use is to be found in the writings of the Reverend W Bingley, who described seeing on the Dyfi in 1798 'two of the boats called coracles, ... these are used chiefly in fishing; they are 5-6 feet long and 3 or 4 broad, of an oval shape and so light that one man may with ease carry them on his shoulders'. He went on to observe that they were originally covered with animal hide, but 'they are now usually covered with pitched canvas. They hold only a single person, who can row himself with incredible swiftness with a paddle in his right hand whilst with the other he can manage a net..'

Another clergyman, The Reverend Richard Warner, writing in *Through Wales in August 1797* said:

> We passed the Dovey which flows to the north of Machynlleth and it divides it from Merionethshire, over an old stone bridge, from which we were gratified by a sight entirely new to us, the management of coracles and the mode of fishing from them ... The coarse pitched canvas having [been substituted as a coating] for it in the room of leather. Intended to carry only one person each, they are not more than 5 feet long and 4 broad, rounded at the corners, and constructed of wicker work; and are consequently sufficiently light to be conveyed on the back of the fisherman to his home, when the labour of the day is concluded ... The man who manages the coracle is seated [in] the centre of it, and directs its motion by the action of a small paddle, with which it is truly astonishing how he commands this apparently awkward vessel. Two coracles usually go together in order to assist each fishing; and operation of singular address and activity; the right hand being employed all the time in paddling, the left hand in conducting the net, and teeth in holding the line attached to it.

ABERYSTWYTH CORACLES

The evidence of coracle use in this area is tenuous. The print (Plate 28) entitled *Salmon fishery, a view from the rocks of Aberystwith and the Bay of Aberystwith*, drawn and engraved by J Hassel, shows two coracles. The Bay shown is not recognisable, nor can the cottage precariously perched on the top of the cliff be identified, but the presence of the bathing huts suggests it is close to Aberystwyth. Michael Freeman, Curator of the Ceredigion Museum, informed me in 2007 that as far as he knew, bathing huts were to be found only at Aberystwyth at the time. Lewis Morris mentions that salmon were found in the river Rheidol in 1755 but 'not as good as those found in the river Teify'. Despite extensive research it has not proved possible to discover any written evidence of coracle usage on either the Rheidol or the Ystwyth. This does not, of course, mean that coracles were not used in the area. Similarly neither Hornell or Jenkins were aware of the existence of coracle usage on the river Dwyryd in north Wales, but as will appear later in this chapter, there is clear evidence of such usage.

CORACLES ON THE UPPER SEVERN AND FYRNWY

It has already been stated that the Severn in its heyday had more coracles on it than any other river in Great Britain. It is also distinguished by the fact that it has no less than four quite different types of coracle used on its waters. Consideration has already been given to those found in the English areas of Shrewsbury, Ironbridge and Bewdley, but equally important are the craft which would have been encountered in times past on or near to the Welsh section of the Severn.

Welshpool

There are four main sources of information about these coracles, namely A. Stanley Davies, Hornell, Jenkins, and Brian Waters's book *Severn Stream* (1949). It is not clear exactly when any of their sources of information were obtained.

Stanley Davies' information came primarily from an interview in 1935-6 with Samuel Phillips of Leighton Bridge, Welshpool, then aged 78. Samuel was a native of Trewern, a Severnside township opposite Pool Quay at the foot of the Breiddens. He described how he, his father and grandfather had all made and used coracles for net fishing in the same general manner as is practised in west Wales. Net fishing with coracles on the Severn in Wales ceased in 1890. After that date he related that his coracle was used for setting night lines until that practice was also declared illegal. Finally, he said that the last use of his coracles was for the retrieving of ducks that had been shot.

At the time he spoke to Stanley Davies, Samuel Phillips explained that the next pair of coracles to his family's were at Criggion opposite Llandrinio bridge and were owned by a Mr Weston and a man by the name of Lowndes, a gamekeeper for the owner of Breidden Forrest.

Samuel Phillips gave a clear and succinct account of how his coracles were made and used:

> ... the Trewern type of coracle has no sheer; if any sheer were given to the fore end it would be difficult to pull in a salmon out of the net. It is 4 ft 9 inches long by 3 ft 3 inches wide and 18 inches deep at the seat. The pointed end is the stern and is called the back. The bow is called the fore end. The centre of the seat is two feet away from the back. The user sits facing the fore end. The frame is made of Ash, riven by hand with a hoop shaver (a cooper's tool). The slats are one and a half inches by a quarter inch. The interwoven framework is made of 7 slats lengthways and 8 slats broadways with a short slat added to each corner.
>
> The coracle is made as follows: an old door is placed on the ground. The slats are laid on and interwoven, and each nailed in two places to the door. Only slats which have been riven can be interwoven. If the modern method of using sawn laths is adopted the laths must be nailed together with copper nails. The ends of the slats are then softened with hot water and bent up to meet the inside rim of the gunwale. The slats are then nailed to the gunwale. The nails should be flat headed clog nails, as they are soft enough to be clinched, but they are difficult to obtain. The gunwale is of ash and is 13 feet 4 inches long. Owing to the difficulty of obtaining such a long length, it can be in two pieces which meet under the seat. In addition, four slats are laid on the bottom of the coracle to take the pressure of the user's feet. There are also two round pieces of timber one inch in diameter, one end of which is screwed to the under side of the seat and the other end to the bottom of the coracle to distribute the weight of the seat. The frame is then covered with calico, and waterproofed inside and out with a mixture of 2 pounds of pitch and one pound of tar. The outer rim of the gunwale is then nailed on. Two short strips are nailed to the gunwale to help support the seat. The seat is 8 inches wide and is fixed last of all. Alongside the left hand side of the seat is kept the 'priest', a stout oak stick about one foot long used for stunning the salmon. It is hung just below the gunwale in two loops of leather.
>
> The paddle, 4 feet 3 inches long, has the edges of one side of the blade chamfered, this side must be kept 'next to the water' which you are drawing towards you; otherwise you will find yourself out of the coracle and in the water...

He went on to describe the manner in which the coracle was carried. It should be noted that every other English or Welsh coracle, with the exception of those in the Welshpool, upper Dee, and Conwy areas has a strap which is set in the seat through which the coracles user's shoulders are inserted. Phillips explained his method of carrying his coracles thus: 'I prefer to carry the coracle horizontally and inverted, lifting it up and letting the flat of the seat rest on the left shoulder; then I place the paddle on my right shoulder, and let the blade fit under the seat to take part of the weight. The net is thrown over the top (really the inverted bottom of the coracle) which avoids the user getting wet from the net. If you carry the coracle on your back by means of a strap looped to the seat the wind is liable to fill the coracle and blow you off your feet.' From this description, a replica Welshpool coracle was made by me and my son-in-law Graham Crerar. It was given to the Welshpool Museum (Plate 29).

Stanley Davies was also told by a 73-year-old man, David Ruscoe, then of Welshpool but formerly of Llandrinio, that he had often seen Criggion coracles operating. He recalled that although the 'modern' material from which laths were made was ash, 'the frame work of the coracles I saw were made out of strong briars pulled from the hedgerow.' It will be recalled that the late Jack Davies of Shrewsbury remembered briars being similarly used on the Shrewsbury stretch of the Severn.

Hornell's informant, whom he interviewed in 1935, was also named Samuel Phillips and, unquestionably, the same man as Davies had interviewed. Indeed their historical accounts are identical, but Hornell's version of the construction of the coracle in question whilst covering the same ground is more technical.

Interestingly Hornell refers to Davies having made further enquires since they had last met. This revealed that 'several old men testified to the fact that William Evans of Haimwood, Llandrinio, the last coracleman on the reach below Criggion and on the last reach of the river Fyrnwy before it joins the Severn, made the framework of his coracles of strong briars pulled from the hedgerows. Coracle fishermen were often poor and would not buy material if a substitute could be obtained free'. The reference to coracles on the river Fyrnwy is interesting as an indication of how widespread coracle usage was in Wales in earlier times.

Jenkins adds nothing further to what was described by Hornell.

Brian Waters' book provides a wonderfully evocative account of the Severn and the countryside surrounding it, and the people who lived and worked close to or on it. When talking about the Pool Quay area near Welshpool he gives a description of a remarkable voyage by a Severn waterman who travelled by coracle from Pool Quay to Lundy Island: it took him a fortnight to complete the round trip.

He also recounts how when an engraver wished to travel from Buttington to Shrewsbury by river with some of his engravings he was offered the services of a local coracleman – which he perhaps too hastily declined, because two short periods of carrying one's coracle would have meant a shorter time than could have been achieved by boat!

Like Davies and Hornell, Brian Waters met a local coracleman who was then 83. He had been born at Trewern Farm and was also named Phillips, but, in his case, with a forename of Griff. He told Brian Waters it was nearly sixty years since he and his brother fished with a net for salmon between two coracles. He said the net they had used had a 5" mesh, was 12 yards long and 6-8" deep. It was weighted at the bottom, and the top was fastened to a line of cow horn rings, 18 inches apart. The fishing technique he described was broadly similar to that in use on the coracle rivers of west Wales today.

In common with Bernard Thomas, the Llechryd Teifi coracleman, Phillips described to Waters how he rescued a horse from a flood area. He also described how he used his coracle to lay night lines when net fishing by coracle was prohibited, and explained how he did so. He went on: 'The prohibition of coracle netting was the beginning of the decline in coracle making. Sixty years ago coracles could be counted in scores, where they are found now only singly along the Severn. I doubt if today there are as many as a dozen coracles in use along the Severn or more than twice that number in existence'. His description of how coracles were made was very similar to that described by Hornell and Davies.

Reconciling these accounts presents problems. One assumes that the Phillipses referred to are at least related, but this is not stated, and the actual relationship can only be a matter of conjecture. Hornell states in which year he interviewed his informant, but neither Davies nor Waters do so. As all three of them spent a considerable time with their informants, possible errors of first names can be discounted. Be that as it may, there can be no doubt that the upper Severn had a substantial coracle heritage in the eighteenth and nineteenth centuries.

THE CORACLES OF THE DEE

The Dee coracles are particularly important, as they were the last coracles to be used in north Wales. When Welsh coracles are discussed today, thoughts automatically turn to the rivers of west Wales, and yet it is on the great northern river, the Dyfrdwy, or as it is known in English, the Dee, where most coracles were found, and which Hornell regarded as the most important of all north Wales rivers. Dee coracles were divided into two very distinct types, differing from each other in size, capacity, construction, use and history: the lower Dee, or Bangor, coracles, and the upper Dee, or Llangollen, coracles.

Lower Dee Coracles
Thomas Pennant stated in *Tours in Wales* in 1810 that Dee coracles were much used for salmon fishing and were no longer covered with hide 'but with pitched canvas. They hold only a single person, who uses a paddle with great dexterity'.

Fig 4 : 10
Lower Dee coracles in Bangor Is-coed near Wrexham during floods.

144

The Dean of Chester, J. S. Howson DD, writing in 1870 about the Dee in Wales, refers to the coracles to be found there, which cost £2 to make and which were used for net fishing for salmon as well as 'ferrying across the river'. He went on to say that it was lower Dee coraclemen who almost always won the races for coracles at Chester. He also recounted meeting two coraclemen returning from fishing walking towards Overton with their coracles on their backs.

Correspondence dated 1891 in the Museum of Welsh Life Archive (MWL MS 971) records that there were about twelve coracles at Bangor Is-coed (see Fig. 4:10), with the same number at Holt, a few at Erbistock, and one or two on Llyn Tegid, near Bala. Furthermore, other correspondents in the same archive dated 1903 indicated that by then there were eleven pairs of coracles at Bangor, only three of which were then allowed for fishing. So it is apparent that by then the numbers of coracles had begun to decline. Hornell records that by 1920 the three remaining nets worked by three pairs of coracles were bought out by the Dee Fishery Board for a sum of £1,000, raised by subscription from riparian landowners (those whose land includes a length of riverbank). This was the culmination of a restrictive process whereby no new licences had been granted when any had lapsed by death, so that the six Bangor men were the last stumbling block to a clear river so far as netting was concerned.

N.B. Precisely the same thing happened at Cenarth on the Teifi in much more recent times, but without any compensation being paid. One of the six was a man named James Johnson, who made coracles as well as using them. During the closed season he used to make baskets, which developed, after coracle net-fishing had ceased, into a substantial business which is still carried onto this day by his descendents at Bangor Is-coed.

Method of Net Fishing

Hornell pointed out that the technique employed was very similar to that in use on the rivers of west Wales although the lower Dee net was heavier.

Another Museum of Welsh Life archive (No MWL MS 3253) records how the lower Dee coracle netsmen started at Crook of Dee (not far from Chester) and worked down in stretches, a certain time

Fig 4 : 11
Lower Dee coracles in the Museum of Welsh Life.

being allowed for each stretch. A second pair then started the next stretch. The coracles were then carried back to the starting point. Moreover, an article which appeared in the *Wrexham Leader* dated 25 June 1982 also dealt with the demise of coracle netting on the lower Dee. In it the writer stated that the right to fish with coracles 'had been practiced at Bangor since time immemorial and the right to ply a coracle was usually hereditary'. The same article also confirmed what Hornell said about how the end of net fishing came about, adding that the buying out of the right to fish previously described had been carried out amicably. The Museum of Welsh Life archive (already referred) to also mentioned the part played by the Vicar of Bangor in protecting the rights of the older fishermen.

The late Harry Stant was so attached to his lower Dee coracle (Fig. 4:11) that he built a shed for it in his garden at Bangor Is-coed, where it was seen by Hornell in 1935 who recorded its dimensions and method of construction, as well as photographing it. Happily it was finally secured for the National Museum of Wales, and now forms part of the celebrated coracle collection at the Museum of Welsh Life at Cardiff.

The lower Dee coracle differs from all other British coracles in the following ways:

1. It has a greater number of laths.
2. These laths are much narrower and thinner than those found in other coracles.
3. There is a stout median strut which runs from the seat to the stern gunwale. (This is also found in the upper Dee coracle but in no other).
4. It has no less than six gunwale strips.
5. The great bulge of its tumble-home sides.
6. Its elegant long paddle which has a notched iron band at its top for carrying purposes.

Hornell describes this coracle as follows:

> The shape in plan is that of an ellipse slightly pinched in, waist like, on the sides. The fore end is regularly curved; the stern curve distinctly flattened ... the prominence of the deep bilge on either side gives a beam nearly 9 inches greater close to the bottom than on the gunwale.
>
> The framework is formed of interlaced laths locally called 'splints'. These are exceptionally slender, so, to compensate for this, the transverse laths are greatly increased in number and the majority are arranged in compound sets, each set corresponding to one of the transverse laths seen in south Wales coracles. There are 9 longitudinal laths or frames, set 4 or 5 inches apart; in the front compartment forward of the seat, each of the five central ones is strengthened by a pair of foot splints, short accessory laths, one on each side to protect the bottom under the paddler's feet. The transverse frames number 8. The forward three are compound, composed respectively, counting from before backwards, of three, four and five laths. The next three in the seat region are single, while the two aftermost ones are composed of two and three laths respectively.
>
> The gunwales are formed of lath hoops in two series, an upper and lower; the seat is inserted between the two so that it is set about an inch below the upper surface of the gunwale which has the

appearance of being reflected over the ends of the seat. A lattice work partition, having a median stout pillar, is fitted under the seat and divides the interior into two unequal compartments – a fore compartment, 33 inches long and an after one, 24 inches in length ... A paddle, a carrying strap of the usual type, and a thong loop passed around the central pillar below the seat are the only accessories.

The paddle is 5 feet long and of unusual elegance, the blade and loom are of equal length; the blade tapers evenly from the broad distal end, and were it not for the merest trace of shouldering, would merge insensibly into the cylindrical loom. No crutch is present; in its place we find the end of the loom encircled by an iron band, notched and slotted at one side. When the owner slings the coracle on his back, he passes the end of the loom through the thong loop past round the seat pillar; the notch serves to prevent the loop slipping off ...

Construction

The two sets of laths which are to form the frame work are arranged as usual on the ground or preferably on a wooden flooring where they are kept in relative position after interlacing by weights or tacking down. The ends of the transverse laths on one side are then bent up and locked between two stiff rods running longitudinally, each lath end being tied to the embracing rods. The lath ends on the opposite side are similarly treated; this done, the ends of the two opposed rods are connected by cords at the distance apart which is to be the eventual width of the coracle at gunwale level. The ends of the longitudinal laths are similarly treated and held in place by cords running fore and aft. The result is that the frame work appears of the form of a rectangular basket work trough with four sides not joined together at the corners. To facilitate bending, the laths are sometimes thinned at the bends.

When the curved laths are sufficiently set, the lattice work seat partition is placed in position and wired at several points along the bottom edge to the laths below. This done, the two lower gunwale hoops are nailed in position, one outer and the other inner to the laths and about an inch and a half below what will be the eventual gunwale edge. The ends of the laths embraced by the paired rods are now released and the seat may be put in, its ends passing over and beyond the lower gunwale hooping. The ends of three of the transverse lathes are passed through slots in each end, a procedure which causes the waist like appearance when the coracle is completed. The seat is further secured by being wired at intervals through paired holes to the upper edge of the partition below. The upper gunwale hoops are next added, one on each side of the projecting frame ends which are now cut off flush. These upper hoops pass over the seat ends.

The coracle is then ready to be covered with calico. The edges are reflected over the gunwale and tacked on. After receiving a coating of the usual pitch and tar mixture, an extra inner gunwale hoop is added to hide and protect the turned-in edge of the cover.

Dimensions of lower Dee coracles are given in Appendix 1

When all the coracles and allied craft described in this book are ultimately considered, the lower Dee coracle must be rated one of the most beautiful to have evolved, and it is all the more tragic that its existence was prematurely brought to an end in the way that it was.

UPPER DEE (LLANGOLLEN) CORACLES

It may seem somewhat artificial to consider coracle usage on the upper and lower Dee separately, but it will become apparent that there are substantial dissimilarities between upper and lower Dee coracles.

The upper Dee coracle differs from its sister craft in its general shape, construction, development, usage, reasons for its decline, and better recording of its personalities. Each will be considered in turn.

Hornell describes how the two types of Dee coracles differ from one another. A comparison of the lower Dee coracle now in the possession of the Museum of Welsh Life (Fig. 4:11) and the 'Whitworth' upper Dee coracle (also in the Museum of Welsh Life) (Fig. 4:12) confirms Hornell's account visually.

Incidentally, it is interesting to note how the 'Whitworth coracle' came to be in the Museum. I discovered this coracle when it was in the possession of a 90-year-old lady, Mrs Patti Ll. Whitworth of Bryn Oerog, Trefor, near Wrexham. It had been made for her late husband and despite being nearly a hundred years old was in pristine condition. At my suggestion she agreed to donate it to the Museum of Welsh Life.

General shape

Hornell wrote that the chief differences to be noted in the Llangollen coracle are:

1. The use of broader lathes (planed ash); nine run fore and aft and sixteen crosswise – nine forward of the seat, three under it, and four abaft it.
2. The presence of a short diagonal lath at each corner
3. Two rows of pillars support the seat, one under the fore edge, the other under the after edge. Each row consists of seven stout, squared pillars with the ends recessed into a lower and upper transverse bar.
4. The emphatic shear given to each end.
5. The lateral gunwales show no appreciable pinching in amidships; the two end ones are nearly straight except at the corners, thereby giving the gunwale view a square box-like appearance.
6. No carrying strap present; the customary way of carrying is to support the seat across the shoulders, steadying the coracle with the hands gripping the sides close to the fore end.[5]
7. The paddle is short barely four feet in length, the blade, 22" long, is nearly parallel sided, being 4½" wide under the shoulders and 5" at the outer end. The loom is cylindrical and without crutch. It is clearly shown in photograph Fig. 4:28, showing Sam Roberts and his Llangollen coracle.

In *Fishing Fantasy* (1949), Captain J Hughes Parry, the distinguished Llangollen fisherman, gives a description of a two-seated coracle, as given by Hornell. He also, however, refers at page 19 to single-seated coracles. He writes: 'a single coracle weighs some 30 lbs and a double one some 10 pounds heavier.' He does not suggest that single coracles were of a different design to the two-seated variety. Here it is interesting to note that another renowned Dee fisherman, whose family had used coracles for angling on the Dee in the Llangollen area for very many years, Neil Graesser, who corresponded with me in 1990, wrote: 'the ones I used were always square and not sloped profoundly at all ... We had a very big working coracle ... which was deeper, a two-man coracle for fishing accompanied by a ghillie, and a one-man coracle. *All were very much the same model*' [Italics mine – to

Fig 4 : 12
The 'Whitworth' upper Dee coracle in the Museum of Welsh Life.

emphasise that all were of the same construction, if not the same
size.]

Moreover, David C Jones of Llangollen, a member of an upper
Dee coracling family, wrote me a letter in the 1990s in which he
mentioned that his family had a single as well as a double coracle.
Whilst double upper Dee coracles remain, there is not a one-seated
upper Dee coracle in existence.

Hornell, however, refers to two old coracles in use for pike
netting on Llyn Tegid, Bala, as well as angling on the Dee. He writes:
'they resemble closely the Bangor Is-coed type except that both
possess short diagonal corner laths and are without the wide bilge
common to the Llangollen and Bangor designs. I am inclined to
think that originally when netting was common, wherever possible
along the whole course of the Dee the type in use was that of the Bala
coracle, more nearly related of the two to the Bangor type; if so the
wide bilge of the present day would be a later modification ... This
particular Bala coracle is of a very old type ... (weighing) ... 86 lbs.'
He attributed this unusual weight to the possibility that the coracles
cover was of flannel. (It will be remembered that coracles were
covered in flannel in west Wales before calico and canvas were used.)

Hornell's theory that the Bala coracle was the forerunner of the
Llangollen and Bangor coracles would appear to be supported by the

fact that at one time the Welsh Dee was a free river, which subsequently became restricted as to use. It is suggested that the upper Dee coracle in its more recent form was the product of this restricted usage, whereby only a limited number of people became eligible to fish the Dee in the Llangollen area, as will become apparent later.

Construction and development

Again we are indebted to Hornell for clear descriptions of a typically wooden-framed upper Dee coracle, and an aluminium-framed variant which was developed towards the end of the Llangollen coracle's life. He writes:

> ... the method of constructing both the wooden and the aluminium frame coracles is practically identical. The following is that of a wooden-framed one.
>
> After two sets of laths have been interlaced in the usual manner on a plank flooring, a wooden roller about 3 feet long by about 6 inches diameter, having an iron pin running through it, is placed lengthwise over the laths on each side and secured to the floor by iron brackets ... the two rollers are arranged at a distance apart of about what the eventual gunwale beam is to be. Discarded rollers from an old mangle are suitable for this purpose. The projecting parts of the transverse laths, after a preliminary soaking with warm water, are bent up and tacked against the upper part of the rollers on the outer aspect, their ends sloping inwards to form the tumble-home type of side characteristic of this design. After being left for sometime to set the bends, the projecting ends, at the proper level are nailed between a pair of lower gunwale hoops, each composed of two half hoops, in the Bangor manner, but instead of being arranged horizontally, the half hoops are fixed with such a shear towards the end of the framework that their ends cross one another obliquely amidships. The two rollers are now removed and the seat with its two sets of pillar supports are put in and secured in place; this permits of the nailing on of the upper circumferential hoops to form the gunwale proper. A cover of sail cloth is stretched over the frame; an overlap at each corner strengthens what are the weakest places. The aluminium framed coracle is made in the same way except that at each intersection of the laths in the framework, the two strips are riveted together and that the aluminium laths do not require to be tacked to the bilge forming rollers.

> The stability of these coracles is such that a man may sit almost on
> the gunwale without causing a capsize. (Hornell, 1938)

Dimensions of upper Dee coracles are given in Appendix 1.

Returning to the upper Dee paddle, A. G. Bradley, in his 1915 book
Clear Water, which will be referred to in some detail later, mentions
that the Llangollen coracle's paddle 'is a short one-bladed paddle'.

The size and shape of the upper Dee paddle suggests that it
would only have been used with one and not two hands. This view is
reinforced in correspondence I have had with David Maybury, the
grandson of the famous professional Dee angler and coracle-handler,
the late George Maybury. Referring to his father, also a Dee
coracleman, David wrote: 'My Dad was never seen by myself
handling a craft with more than one hand except when he lifted it
from the water.'

Usage

Happily there is an abundance of material concerning the use of
coracles on the upper Dee. As has already been mentioned, these
coracles were used for the netting of pike on Llyn Tegid, Bala. In a
letter dated 5 June 1996, Mrs S. G. Dilley, a resident in Llangollen
from 1949 until 1960, described how a coracle 'was used regularly by
a man to cross the river Dee to his allotment on the further bank (by
this means he had a shorter walk than over Llangollen bridge.) On
his decease the coracle apparently was on show in a Welsh
showroom by the mill for many years'.

By far and away the most important use of coracles on the upper
Dee was in connection with angling. Hornell, when discussing
Llangollen coracles, cites 'the advantages for angling on a rocky
shallow river of a coracle over any other craft'. In particular, he draws
attention to its very shallow draught, manoeuvrability, and ability to
remain motionless when required.

Jack Hughes-Parry was renowned not only for his considerable
angling skills, but also for his ability to handle a coracle in the most
difficult of water conditions. He writes as follows: 'a coracle is almost
a necessity on the rough rocky middle reaches of the Welsh Dee,
where owing to the force of the current and deep hidden ledges and

clefts in the rocky bottom, wading is impossible in many places and no other type of craft, not even a birch bark canoe can possibly be used.' He takes the matter further when he states: 'It is possible to shoot rapids and dodge in between out-jutting ledges in the fastest and wildest streams, holding on by gaff or paddle to some outcropping ledge or rock, and one can tuck oneself in perfect safety with a rush of wild white water on each side. By using a coracle one can therefore fish places that could never be reached either by wading or throwing the longest line from the bank.'

Another advantage of using an upper Dee coracle for rod and line fishing is that fish do not appear to have the slightest fear of the craft, according to Hughes Parry. He observes that a further advantage is provided for the angler by the use of a coracle when he states that 'much finer and lighter tackle can also be used, as the drag of a coracle against even a fairly strong stream is so slight that it is almost impossible for the wildest and strongest salmon to break a cast leader or line, which would snap like a thread if you were fishing off the bank'. Finally, Hughes Parry describes a practice exercised on the upper Dee. He writes: 'Once the fisherman has hooked the salmon from a coracle, unless in very rapid water all he has to do is just to tighten up on the fish and allow it to tow the coracle about'.

It should be noted here that there is no wholly indisputable evidence that two-seated upper Dee coracles were used for net fishing except on Llyn Tegid, Bala, but the coracles used there appear more to resemble Lower rather than upper Dee coracles in construction. However, Geraint Jenkins, quoting a witness to the Commissioners on Salmon Fisheries in 1861, states that 'in the nineteenth century coracle netting was undoubtedly widely practised on the Dee especially in the upper reaches of the river'. The witness's evidence, however, is silent on the precise location, and at its highest hints at a very early practice which latterly was confined to the lower Dee.

There is copious evidence of Llangollen coracles being used by two people, namely an angler and a coracle-handler. In all the other Welsh rivers where coracles were used it was by a single person, with the exception of the Conwy. What made the upper Dee different is that the river banks were owned by a small number of wealthy riparian owners, so that when they and their guests fished on the upper reaches of the Dee they did so very frequently with the assistance of an experienced coracle-handler, who often made the journey from his home to the river by train bringing his coracle with him. This practise is described graphically and humorously by A. G. Bradley, who tells of catching trout from a coracle on the rapid waters of the Dee in the Llangollen area before the First World War. He writes as follows: 'When I first embarked Evan Evans was the only licensed 'Cwrwgl' man on the water and both he and his craft abode at Llangollen. His procedure then, like that of his successors today, was to come up with his coracle by the morning train to Carrog station, and there 200 yards away on Llansaintffraid bridge, to find his fare awaiting him.' He went on to explain that the angler and the coracleman sit side by side on the coracle seat and how the coracleman wields a short bladed paddle, the handle of which is pressed into his armpit while the blade is worked with one hand mainly underwater; the figure of eight being the normal stroke.'

There then follows an intriguing account of how Evan Evans converted from extreme conviviality on the water to total abstinence, following one of his angling passengers, a notable radical MP, having ended up in the river, which brought the local angling association, which licensed Evans, into play. Apparently it was due to their advice that the unfortunate coracleman became a tee-totaller, although he stoutly maintained that the incident was not due to his lack of sobriety but to the manner of the polititian's having lunched before embarking.

When A. G. Bradley went fishing in Evans' coracle he took with him 'a short stiffish rod of 8 or 9 feet, a cast not too fine and three flies.' They would travel for seven or eight miles in the coracle, fishing all the way, until they came to a point near Berwyn Station where Evan Evans and his coracle could return home by train. Bradley added, 'The aim of the coraclist is to run down sideways so that the angler is casting crosswise with the stream whilst the pilot checks the pace at which we should naturally run'. He concludes that 'In high water, too, there is an element of excitement in running some of the rapids, if you look at it that way. But when Evans, after surveying the angry surge and crowding rocks both above and below, all of which he knew by heart, used to say, 'I try it whatefer', one gripped the side of the coracle, gave a thought to the radical MP, and held tight. It was astonishing how he would lift the little tub-shaped craft this way and that as it rocked and rolled and heaved along its apparently perilous course among the bolders'. Later in his book, Bradley describes fishing with one Griffiths, Evan Evans' successor. He stressed, however, that there was a serious shortage of experienced coracle-handlers on the upper Dee at the time about which he was writing.

Tavener in *Salmon Fishing* (1931), quotes, in turn, from an account of fishing on the Welsh Dee by one George Agar Hansard in 1834. He records this account as follows: 'At some time Hansard had been in the valley of the Dee and had seen coracle fishing. He relates how the natives fish from these with a line only a half as long as the rod and how salmon 8 or 10 lbs in weight, have been frequently killed out of coracles without one [viz. a reel],' but Tavener adds, 'He forgot to mention that in playing a salmon the coraclemen would probably follow the fish down as I have often seen during the last 10 years.'

In 1987, a fishery consultant, Neil W. Graesser, earlier mentioned, wrote an authoritative book entitled *Advanced Salmon Fishing: Lessons from Experience* which contained a chapter devoted specifically to fishing from coracles on the Welsh Dee in the Llangollen area. Furthermore, he and I corresponded at some length in 1990 and 1991. Together, the book and the correspondence give a unique insight into Llangollen coracle usage within living memory.

Graesser's grandfather and father owned the Argoed Hall water on the Dee from approximately 1860 to 1955. During that time, for a period of twenty-seven years, Graesser fished from coracles with rod and line, as did his father. Their beat was near Froncysllte, midway between Llangollen and Chirk. Its upstream boundary was the old mill at Plas yn Pentre Farm and it extended downstream to the aquaduct carrying the canal across the valley. There were five main pools on the beat, the first two being fished by coracle only, whilst the other three could be fished either from the bank or by coracle.

In answer to a general question concerning his experience of coracle fishing on the Welsh Dee, Graesser, in a letter written in 1990, replied as follows:

> Firstly this river was ideally suited to coracle fishing for two main reasons. 1. The river was either heavily wooded with mature

deciduous woods encroaching close to the bank of many of the main pools, all the banks were tree lined with fine old hardwood trees. In either case, these trees often impeded casting clearance for the bank fishermen, but the problem could be easily overcome when these pools were fished from a coracle, positioned a short distance out. 2. Many of these pools had an interesting flat rock formation which shelves and protruded a considerable distance out into the deep water of the pool from one or other bank. At low water these soft rock outcrops were often high and dry, but at medium or high water fishing levels they were covered by 1–3 feet of water. The fish sometimes lay close to these, as the shelves were often undermined at their outward point, although it was often possible to wade down these rock ledges, and fish the pool comfortably by doing so, this method was seldom successful, I believe because this caused too much vibration and the fish were disturbed. If on the other hand, one positioned one's coracle and floated over these rock outcrops, using a spiked staff to hold it in position to enable the angler to cast, it caused no disturbance and proved very successful. The handler could let the coracle down two yards after the angler had covered his water from each position. If when he reached the tail of the pool, he wished to fish it down again, he merely landed, lifted the coracle onto his back, walked up to the head of the pool and relaunched. If on the other hand he wished to move on down, he merely shipped his spiked staff on board, and by use of the paddle, moved out into the river and shot the rapids into the next pool downstream without any problem.

We often used to walk to the head of the beat, in the morning, with the coracle on our backs, and spend the entire day fishing from the coracle, slowly working from pool to pool. The fish and tackle were carried in the coracle, and apart from coming to shore to land fish, lunch, or fish a pool down again, we were afloat the whole day.

Graesser explained that until 1947 when his father's last coracle-handler, Robert Jones, died, they fished in the way described above, with Jones as the expert handler. In his book he refers specifically to Jones, describing him as a master craftsman who made his own coracles, adding that 'there were few who could handle one better.' He described how 'He was always immaculately dressed in a heavy tweed jacket with waistcoat out of which hung the chain of his fob watch. He wore well cut breeches, pinkish brown in colour with leather gaiters and highly polished hobnail boots and the whole was surmounted by a green or brown felt trilby hat, the band of which was adorned by several favoured fishing flies'. He added: 'When we arranged to go fishing he was always waiting for us by the seat in front of the summer house at the bottom of the steps which led down from the house, with his 7 ft long gaff and rubber- lined carpenters bag, which he used for carrying the fish, beside him. He would have my father's rod all ready for him, with the gut cast soaking just off the breakwater, while upstream the coracle lay waiting, resting 4 ft off the ground on the wooden platform with the paddle and staff beside it.'

Also during the correspondence, Neil stated in a letter dated 5 December 1990 : 'At the point where we landed with the coracle, there were wooden parallel rails some 4 or 5 ft off the ground on which the coracle was placed, upside down, at the end of the day's fishing. This enabled the coracle handler to bend and then raise himself up with the coracle on his back and walk to where he wished to launch it each day, a far easier method than having to lift it up onto his back which he would otherwise have to do if it had merely been left on the ground. Many of these stances are still in evidence, in several places I know on the river, even to this day'.

Such a sensible arrangement has not been encountered on any other river, but then the two-seated Llangollen coracle is much heavier than most other coracles.

Neil Graesser explained that the water at Argoed was only fished occasionally during the Second World War. He went onto say that when Robert Jones died shortly after the war, they had no-one who could handle the coracle properly. He believed that 'this is a common experience on many of the best beats of rivers which were formally fished from a coracle.'

Neil Graesser, Tom Hughes-Parry (the son of the legendary J Hughes-Parry) and David Maybury agreed that nearly all the proprietors of the river bank in the Llangollen area fished from two-seated coracles which were handled by experienced coraclemen. The names of these riparian owners included Sir Henry Robertson and his son Duncan of Llantysilio Hall; Captain J Hughes-Parry of Fechan; Lord Newborough DSC, of Rhug, Corwen; Major P.C. Ormord MC, of Pen y Lan, Rhuabon and Martin Whitworth of Bryn Oerog, Trevor.

History

There is little doubt that coracles have been used on the Dee since very early times, but the practice mentioned earlier involving anglers being carried in one coracle by an expert coracle-handler is a later development albeit in evidence before the First World War. In general terms it had come to an end by the late 1940s, due principally to a lack of expert coracle-handlers.

Geographical boundaries

Hornell asserts: 'The range of this coracle extends from Bala to some distance below the mouth of the river Ceirog with its centre at Llangollen.' Support for this proposition can be found in the Museum of Welsh Life archive previously mentioned in this chapter, in the letter written in 1891, in which it is stated that coracles were to be found on the upper Dee from Farndon upwards, on Llyn Tegid near Bala, and as far down as Erbistock and Bangor Is-coed.

Personalities

Few stretches of river have produced so many well-recorded skilled coracle fisherman and handlers. Mention has already been made of Neil Graesser and all the riparian owners and their handlers, probably the most notable of whom was the late Captain J Hughes-Parry. To this list must be added the names of Isaac Roberts, whose photograph appears in Hornell's book already mentioned; Sam Roberts, who served the Bryn Oerog family as a coracleman (Fig. 4:13), and George Maybury (Fig. 4:14).

When George Maybury died in October 1918, the *Llangollen Advertiser* of 25 October 1918 said: 'By the death of George Maybury ... has removed one of the latest if not the last of a noted group of noted anglers ... Some dozen years ago, the professional angler was a familiar figure to sportsmen who, with rod and line, visited Llangollen. As the coracle and historic bridge now his occupation is all but gone, and there are no successors to the race of which George Maybury formed so excellent a type'. Later on in the obituary it is asserted that 'The privilege of whipping the stream and casting a fly have come into relatively few hands, and the professional fisherman is not of their number, yet there are many secrets of the craft, such as the construction and use of coracles, that were cherished by these

Fig 4 : 13
Sam Roberts in an upper Dee (Llangollen) coracle. He was a coracleman
for the Whitworth family of Brynoerog, Trefor.

worthies, and upon which, perchance even the 'complete angler'
can cast no light'. The writer's claim that the art of upper Dee
coracle-making had finished at that time would appear to be
prophetic but premature, but the article's value is that it clearly paints
a picture of an exceptional coracle fisherman.

The upper Dee coracle is particularly important as it is the last
such craft to have been in traditional use in northern Wales.

CORACLES ON THE RIVERS CONWY, LLEDR, LLUGWY AND NEARBY LAKES

Now, the most northerly of all the Welsh coracle rivers will be
considered.

The earliest reference to coracle usage on the Conwy is to be
found in the National Library of Wales, MS 858893, where it is
indicated that coracles were used in considerable numbers from the

Fig 4 : 14
George Maybury (and passenger) fishing on the Fechan, upper Dee, near
Llangollen, circa 1947.

sixteenth century. But Elis Pierce, otherwise known as Elis o'r Nant, writing in the mid nineteenth century in *The Old Fishing Gear of Nant Conwy*, stated that 'The old inhabitants of Nant Conwy possessed fishing skills the like of which had not been seen, as far as I know, beyond that region although various strangers happened to call from time to time, and amongst them the fisheries representatives, one and all proclaimed that they had never seen such original equipment and instruments as the fishing coracles ... of the upper reaches of Nant Conwy'.

Moreover Dafydd Thomas Jenkins referred in 1972 to the visit of Michael Farraday to the Conwy area in 1819. Farraday is reported as saying, 'Here and there on the river we saw fishermen in their coracles; little vessels something like a washing tub squeezed by a door into an oval form; a board is put across the middle on which two men sit, one each way and whilst one paddles the other casts the net'.

Fig 4 : 15
Ioan Glan Lledr in a Conwy coracle.

Two points are to be made as a result of this account: namely, a) that the Conwy coracle, like the upper Dee coracle is essentially a two man craft, and b) that the method of net fishing employed was akin to that used on the river Boyne at Drogheda, and not the method practised in West Wales. In the HMSO report of the hearings before the Commissioners appointed to enquire into the salmon fisheries in England and Wales in 1861, reference is made to the evidence of Dr Owen Roberts, a fisherman (page 205). He was asked in reference to the Conwy if there were any coracle fishing. He is said to have replied, 'They have stopped that now at Llanrwst; there used to be coracles and nets up on the Lledr fisheries but I suppose they were stopped 25 or 30 years ago.' The next question was thus: 'Are there any coracles used at all on the Conwy?', to which his reply was: 'Below Llanrwst, where the tide comes I am not aware that there are; they were only used where the men could land their nets; they never used them below Trefriw'. When asked how far the coracles fished, the witness replied, 'They fished about 7 or 8 miles above the tideway, and a little lower down for Sparlings. I have seen as many as 500 taken at one time in a coracle net. I do not know whether they do that now'.

Elis o'r Nant, already referred to, makes an astonishing observation as follows: 'When Ioan Glan Lledr used to fish Llyn yr Afanc (Conwy river) at those times when his father and others were working and fishing with him, he owned a much larger coracle, some 4 yards or more in length with two benches across for to sit. The double coracle was normally rowed by two dragging the net to catch salmon'. It is difficult to draw reliable conclusions from such a sparse description, but its length and the fact that it was rowed suggests a craft more akin to a curragh than a coracle. Fig. 4:15 is a photograph of Ioan Glan Lledr in the Conwy coracle about a century ago.

Jenkins stated that coracles were widely used on the Conwy until 1914, but very surprisingly Hornell appears not to have had any knowledge of this rich coracle heritage on the river Conwy.

The Conwy coracle itself

Only one remains, and is to be found in the Museum of Welsh Life. It was donated by Owen Goodwin of Betws y Coed, who was licensed to use a coracle on the Lledr as well as the Conwy in 1887.

It is 5' 6" long, with a width of 3' 4" at the seat and 3' 2" at both bow and stern. Its cleft ash laths are unusually wide: 3". They numbered six longitudinally and nine fore and aft. No diagonal laths were present. The gunwale also of cleft ash measured 2" in depth. There was on the outside of the gunwale a hoop similar to those used by coopers for cask-making nailed to the timber, according to Jenkins. Above the fifth cross lath a heavy bulk of timber was nailed and two timbers supporting the seat were nailed on this. The space below the seat did not form a carrying box for fish, as in some coracles, but these pillars were used by the fishermen for carrying the coracles on their heads; the pillars serving as hand grips. It should be noted that no other coracle is or was carried in this manner.

The river Llugwy (and nearby lakes) coracles

According to page 16 of *Traditional Fishing in Wales* (1995), by Emrys Evans, 'Coracles were also used for netting on lakes as well as on rivers. With the coracle it was possible to take the "gwestan" (a line with a single hook) and the "tant" (a line with more than one hook) out from the shore.'

In *The A-Z of Betws-y-coed*, by David Limburn Shaw (1990),

mention is made of coracles being used on the Llugwy river until 1884, and later that 'In 1856 the mussel could be found in the river Conwy for a mile upstream from Llanrwst Bridge to Betws-y-coed and on stretches of the river Llugwy. It was fished from coracles on these waters'.

From the above it will be seen that the Conwy, Lledr, Llugwy and their nearby lakes had a rich and varied coracle heritage.

CORACLES ON THE RIVER DWYRYD

Finally, mention must be made of a unique coracle which is not mentioned in any of the standard works on coracles. The river Dwyryd flows through the vale of Maentwrog in North West Wales and is tidal as far as Maentwrog. For reasons which will appear later there can be little doubt that coracles were used for net fishing on this river. A Dwyryd coracle, which was in the possession of the Sandford family of the Isle Estate, Bicton, Shrewsbury, was first discovered by the traditional Shrewsbury coracle-maker, John E. Davies, in 1986. He used to make his coracles on the premises of a farm on the Isle estate where he and his family paddled their coracles on the river Severn. John Davies told me about it – I was at the time the Chairman of the Coracle Society – and I immediately appreciated its uniqueness. At my request John made an exact replica, which is now on display at the National Coracle Centre, Cenarth, Newcastle Emlyn, west Wales.

I wrote straight away to the Sandfords seeking information about this highly unusual coracle. The late Mrs Sheila Sandford, wife of the then owner of the Isle estate, replied on 9 May. Her letter made it clear that the Sandfords possessed two such coracles. She said, amongst other things, 'we have two similar – the other one is usable, but very slightly. They in fact belonged to my brother in law, who is now Lord de Clifford, and his aunt, a remarkable woman, Mrs Inge. She had them made and [they] were I believe used on the estuary of the Dwyryd for netting and paddled from the front. She had a big house, the 'Plas' (now owned by the Gwynedd County Council and used as an environmental centre for the Snowdonia National Park).'

Sheila Sandford suggested that the author contact her father, the late Duncan Robertson, of Llantysilio Hall, Llangollen, whom I knew to be knowledgeable concerning upper Dee coracles. Replying to my letter, Robertson wrote: 'The coracle she has was used on the river at Maentwrog for netting purposes; it is a small craft and only used for crossing the small river and possibly working the net down. I do not know who made it.'

Inquiries were made for evidence of coracle use in the Maentwrog area by Edwyn Roberts, who was brought up locally. On 9 August 1988 he wrote to me, saying, 'I well remember Mrs Inge, who was a formidable lady and local landowner in Maentwrog. She was in fact a daughter of the Oakely family who were quarry owners in Blaenau Ffestiniog. The old boathouse where the coracle almost certainly was kept is still standing, and can be seen on a long bend in the Dwyryd between Maentwrog village and the Plas. I feel certain I heard of the use of a coracle but did not witness its use myself.'

Finally, I was told by an archivist at Gwynedd County Council that he believed that the estate at one time had a salmon netting licence.

It would appear that the use of a coracle for netting fish on the Dwyryd was not by use of two coracles with a net between them, as on the rivers Taf, Teifi and Tywi, but rather used to pay out a net secured to the bank, as was practised on the Boyne in Ireland and on the Severn at Ironbridge.

I visited the late Humphrey Sandford, the husband of the earlier-mentioned Sheila Sandford, shortly before he died. Sandford showed me the original Dwyryd coracle and a second craft which appeared to be a somewhat crude copy of the original. Subsequently Humphrey Sandford gave the original craft to me (as President of the Coracle Society), and I donated it to the Museum of Welsh Life, where it is currently kept (Plate 30).

The Dwyryd coracle is a very unusual craft. The configuration at the bow and stern is not to be found in any other coracle. The only allied craft which is in any way similar so far as the bow is concerned is the Owey Island (Donegal) paddling curragh, which can be seen at the National Coracle Centre.

A relative newcomer to coracle construction is Alan Grove of Kidderminster. He is a highly skilled maker of ancient musical instruments. He made an exact replica of the original Dwyryd coracle. He is of the opinion that it was made on a mould in the same way as the Shrewsbury coracle in the Museum of Welsh Life's collection.

Whilst coracles in use in Wales today can not compare in numbers with those to be found in Vietnam, they are nevertheless important for the following reasons, namely:

1. In no other country is there to be found so many different types of coracles as have been mentioned in this chapter, and
2. It is only in Wales that there have been so many changes in coracle construction over the years, such as the replacement of woven gunwales with those made of ash laths, the replacement of animal hides and flannel by canvas and calico as covers for coracle frames, the use of aluminium in place of ash or willow as laths, and the replacement of natural wood materials by fibre glass.

Notes

[1] J. F. Jones, *Salmon Fisheries 1863*, in the Carmarthenshire Antiquary (1962-3), p. 210.
[2] R. J. Collyer, *The Teifi: Scenery & Antiquities of a Welsh River* (Llandysul, 1987), p. 56.
[3] Sadie Ward, *The Countryside Remembered* (Century Books, 1991).
[4] H. P. Wyndham, A Tour through Monmouthshire & Wales (1781), p. 52.
[5] NB: Later on in the description Hornell states that this method of portage is a comparatively recent innovation and indicates that old photographs such as Fig 4:27 show that the coracle is being carried in the orthodox manner by means of a strap across the coracleman's shoulders.

Chapter Five
EUROPEAN CORACLES

It must now be apparent that in the past there was an abundance of coracles in the United Kingdom and Ireland, and that several types remain. It must be said, however, that of these only a handful are used as working craft.

It is not an unreasonable surmise that coracles must have been in evidence throughout Europe but, sadly, there is little supporting evidence.

The only historical reference to hide-covered craft is to be found in the *Pharsalia of Lucan* (translated by H. T. Riley, 1853). Writing between AD 39 and 65, Lucan, referring to an incident during Julius Caesar's wars in Spain in 49 BC, when his lines of communications had been cut by troops fighting on behalf of Pompey, wrote: '... when the Sicoris regains its banks and leaves the plain, in the first place, the white willows, its twigs in water, is woven into small boats, and covered over, the bullock being slaughtered; adapted for passengers it floats along the swelling stream. Thus does the Venetian on the flowing Padus [the Po] and on the expanded ocean the Briton sail.'

The final reference to 'sailing ... on the expanded ocean' by Britons would suggest that the craft would have been of the curragh variety rather than a coracle. It is also apparent that the craft referred to by Lucan was built as a result of what Caesar had encountered in Britain and, accordingly, was not indigenous to the Lerida area of Spain.

James Hornell wrote as follows: 'Vessels of the type described [i.e. curragh-type craft] employed in coastal fishing and transport, would certainly be better known to foreign travellers and writers than the small coracles used by the natives on the rivers in localities often wild and difficult of access, buried for the most part in the depths of the dense forests that covered so much of the land at that period.' It is submitted that is why there is so little reliable evidence of the existence of European coracles outside of the United Kingdom and Ireland.

There is, however, some evidence of the existence of coracles in latter day Poland, the Ukraine and Norway.

POLISH CORACLES

I am greatly indebted to Witek Glinski of Angarrock, Hayle, Cornwall for telling me about coracles in Poland between 1935 and 1939. Witek lived there until he was forcibly removed from his homeland by the Russians in 1939. He recalls seeing the same bearded elderly man fishing on a lake in a round coracle only large enough to carry one person on a number of occasions. The coracle was constructed 'basket like' in willow with a rounded bottom. It was covered with tarred canvas. Its means of propulsion was a single paddle, about 6' long, 4-5" wide, and made of ash. The coracle drew about 2".

The coracleman fished with a hazel rod about 12' long; his line consisting of 'white horsehair knotted in a special way', and the float was a cork pierced by the quill of a goose feather.

The location of the sighting of this coracle was on a lake known as Czarne Jezioro. It was one of several lakes which had come into existence after many decades of 'uncontrollable burning peat.' It was part of a vast estate and forest owned by a man called Zyberg Plater, who lived some 2 km from Louzki. A highway ran from Louzki to Dzisna. The lake was north of Dzisna and east of the highway. It was close to the border between Poland and Russia formed by the Dzisna (Polish) or Dwina (Russian) river. Witek Glinski stated that the lake was about 600 km from Chernobyl. The significance of this will become apparent later.

Considerable importance is attached to this piece of evidence for two reasons. Firstly, Witek Glinski has for many years made baskets in the UK and has taken a considerable interest in coracles. Accordingly, his description is likely to be very accurate. Secondly, he is a truly remarkable human being, as becomes evident when reading his account of his incredible escape from Siberia to India via Tibet on foot. (He wrote under a pseudonym for security reasons before the overthrow of the Soviet Union.)

I am greatly indebted, too, to Krysztof Zamoecinski MA of the Maritime Ethnology Department of the Polish Maritime Museum of Gdansk, Poland, with whom I corresponded in 2007. Zamoecinski was unable to discover any evidence of coracle construction or usage in contemporary Poland, but there was such usage in the sixteenth century, about which more will be written subsequently.

It would appear, therefore, that the sighting of a coracle by Witek Glinski in Poland before the Second World War was an isolated case.

Zamoecinski's research, however, revealed that skin-covered boats which can be classified as coracles were used in the second part of the sixteenth century by Tatars in Poland. They were small, and their construction consisted of 'tied branches'. They were covered with animal skins.

During the same period craft were used by Zaporozhian Cossacks. In their case they were constructed as '[a] weaved basket resembling [a] Ruthenian cradle'. Zamoecinski goes on to explain that these basket cradles were elongated with rounded ends 'somewhat sharpened with [a] semi-circular longitudinal section', and were covered with either animal hide (probably horse) or oilskin, which was made from waxed cloth in ancient Poland. These craft were called 'chaikas'.

Both Tatar and Cossack coracles were used to cross rivers during military actions.

Finally, Zamoecinski states that '[the] low freeboard of these skin boats made hiding and lurking [easier] in the vicinity of the enemy.'

It is submitted that these craft can fairly be termed 'coracles or allied craft'.

UKRANIAN CORACLES

The evidence in support of the existence of these craft is much less strong. The area referred to is Chernihiv in North of the Ukraine which is some 80 km from Chernobyl, i.e. not far from where the Polish coracle was sighted. The information concerning the possibilities of coracles in the Ukraine is to be found in a letter dated 24 July 1995 from Robert Morgan of Swansea to John Williams Davies, then Honorary Secretary of the Coracle Society. In it, Morgan describes having read an article on coracles in *The Times*. He continued, 'I am currently involved with a number of academic groups in Eastern Europe, including the Kiev Institute of History, and have seen similar craft [presumably coracles] in my work there ... at Chernihiv in the North of Ukraine ... there is evidence of skills including boat-building in the wider sense from cane and reeds'.

NORWEGIAN CORACLES

The position concerning Scandinavia is confusing.

In a letter to me dated 31 August 1989, the then curator of the Powysland Museum in Welshpool, Powys – Eva Bredsdorf, a Scandinavian – stated that she had been in contact with the National Museum of Copenhagen concerning the existence of coracle-like craft in Norway. She stated: 'Apparently there are some reports from the northern part of Norway that a similar boat to a coracle existed in pre-historic time, but the evidence is very uncertain.' She followed this by making enquiries of the Historisk Museum in Bergen, but learnt that they were unaware of coracles or similar craft in Norway.

A view was obtained from a distinguished Norwegian ethnologist, Anne-Berit Borchqrerink, in 1993. She thought there may have been what she termed 'leather boats' in Denmark c. 300 BC and, therefore, it is possible that they could also have existed in Norway. She was of the opinion that the existence of these boats might suggest the use of leather before the use of wood planks, but such a boat would have had a keel and therefore be more akin to a curragh than a coracle.

But the clearest evidence is contained in a letter dated 15 September 1987 from Sir John Nugent of Upper Lambourn, Newbury, Berks. He had earlier stated orally that in the 1950s he had fished on a river close to Trondheim in June. In his letter he described how he 'constantly used the coracle to cross from the Lodge to the other bank of this very fast-flowing river'.

At its highest, the evidence referred to suggests the possibility of coracles having existed in Scandinavia. In the case of Poland to a greater extent, and the Ukraine to a lesser extent, the existence of coracles is more substantially indicated. Sadly, this is the extent of any knowledge about the existence of coracles or similar craft in Europe outside the UK and Ireland.

Chapter Six

MIDDLE EASTERN CORACLES

QUFFAS OF IRAQ

When one turns from Europe to the Middle East there is an abundance of material concerning the usage of coracle-like craft in Iraq until relatively recently. They are known locally as quffas. The first reference to them is found in Herodotus' description of what to him was the most amazing thing in Assyria after Babylon itself. It reads as follows:

> They have boats plying the river down to Babylon which are completely round and are made of leather. In Armenia, which is upstream from Assyria, they cut branches of willow and make them into a frame, around the outside of which they stretch watertight skins to act as a hull; they do not broaden the sides of the boat to form a stern or narrow them into a prow, but they make it round, like a shield. Then they line the whole boat with straw and send it off down the river laden with goods. Their cargo is most commonly palm-wood casks filled with wine. The boats are steered by two men, who stand upright and wield a paddle each; one of them pulls the paddle towards his body and the other pushes the paddle away from his body. These boats vary in size from very large downwards; the largest of them can manage cargo weighing five thousand talents. Each boat carries a live donkey – or, in the case of larger boats, several donkeys. At the end of their voyage to Babylon, when they have sold their cargo, they sell off the frame of the boat and all the straw, load the donkeys up with the skins, and drive them back to Armenia. They do this because the current of the river is too strong for boats to sail up it, and that is why they make these boats out of skin rather than wood. Once they have got back to Armenia with their donkeys, they make themselves more boats in the usual way."

A number of interesting points arise from this detailed description. They are as follows:

1. The shape is similar to the Native American bull boat, Ironbridge coracle, Spey curragh, and one type of Tibetan coracle.

Fig 6 : 1
Quffas near Maud Bridge, Baghdad, from the East Bank, circa 1919.

2. The method of propulsion, namely by pulling the boat forward, is similar to the technique used by bull boats and Donegal paddling curraghs. Both the Boyne curragh and Donegal paddling curragh are, on occasions, propelled by two paddles.
3. The procedure whereby the Quffa is dismantled after primary use is mirrored in an identical practice in Tibet.

Hornell quotes the above mentioned passage from Herodotus, and then is very critical of it. In essence, he alleges that Herodotus, a stranger to the area, has confused the quffa with a kelek. Keleks were large timber rafts supported on several inflated goat skins. He bases his criticisms on the following points:

1. Wine in those days and in that area, he states, was conveyed in large earthenware jars, not in wine casks made of palm wood. He asserts that palms did not grow on the mountains of Armenia. It is observed that wooden cases would be infinitely safer for transport on turbulent rivers than earthenware jars, and it might be that the cases were acquired elsewhere and subsequently used.

2. He states that quffas are useless for heavy cargo work if they have to 'thread rock-beset defiles.' Some of the larger coracles such as Bewdley or Ironbridge coracles are recorded as carrying a number of people at the same time on the Severn, which has rapids at, for instance, Bicton near Shrewsbury.

3. Quffas were not used for traffic from the hill country, says Hornell, during the time he was aware of them, i.e. the early part of the twentieth century. Consequently, they would not have been broken up into their constituent parts and would have been used continuously until they were unserviceable. Here it is observed that Tibetan coracles, as will be seen later, were often dismantled and carried on animals during the return journey.

4. Herodotus described the carrying capacity of a quffa as ranging up to 5000 talents, the equivalent weight of which be between 125 and 175 tons. It may be that Herodotus exaggerated the carrying capacity of a quffa, but it should be remembered that some quffas were unusually large. Additionally, the Donegal paddling curragh, for instance, has a remarkable and unexpected carrying capacity, frequently carrying horses and cattle.

It is of considerable significance that whereas Herodotus describes quffas as being circular – as, in fact, does Hornell himself, the latter, however, goes on to say that keleks 'are often 40 feet square'. It is inconceivable that Herodotus would have been confused about the difference between a circle and a square. In short, whilst there are criticisms which can be made of Herodotus' description, it is submitted that it is unreasonable to discard it completely.

Having been critical of Hornell's comments on Herodotus' description, it must be said that his section headed 'The Coracles of the Tigris and Euphrates' is highly informative, and the most valuable contribution to the study of quffas. Indeed, there is no other description which contains so many useful facts. The only other information I have been able to secure from other sources concerning more recent use of quffas is as follows: I had the advantage of speaking to and corresponding with Glencairn Balfour-Paul CMG, in 2000: he is a former British ambassador in Iraq, having served there from 1969 to 1971.

Glencairn Balfour-Paul stated that he had occasionally seen

quffas being used by fishermen in small numbers on the Tigris during this time. He had not, however, been aware at any time of their having been used on the Euphrates. He attributed their decline to the building of bridges, railways and roads, together with the emergence of river launches. He kindly supplied me with copies of a series of photographs of quffas in and around Baghdad, very early in the twentieth century (Fig. 6:1). These photos had been given to him by an Iraqi friend when the then Ambassador was required to leave the country by its Vice-President, Saddam Hussein.

Glencairn Balfour-Paul also had two quffas made for the now defunct Exeter Maritime Museum (one of which can be seen in a somewhat dilapidated state at the National Coracle Centre in west Wales). They were made by a blind Iraqi woman on the Tigris, some miles south of Baghdad. But he was unable to say if women were the sole quffa makers, as was the case with Native American bull boats.

Wilfred Thesiger in his book *The Marsh Arabs* (1964) wrote thus: 'a circular coracle, called the quffa, used to be common around Baghdad. The furthest south I saw one was below Kut, near Sheikh Saad.' He also made mention of what he refers to as 'an interesting type of coracle, called a 'Zaima''. Apparently, he saw it on one occasion only, on a branch of the Euphrates below Suq ash Shuyukh. It was made of quasab and coated with bitumen. It is feared that Thesiger was using the word 'coracle' very loosely, as the craft measured 10' in length and was 2½ feet at its widest. Moreover, it had a keel. Whilst it was made of bundles of quasab reeds with two or three willow wands, and was covered with bitumen, it can not be regarded as a coracle within the terms of the earlier definition of such a craft.

Hornell gave a good description of the nature and use of a quffa. In *The Coracles of the Tigris and the Euphrates* (1938) he wrote: 'In shape a quffa is almost identical with the Tibetan coracle of the Yalung river, the craft likened in form to the Tibetan food bowl – perfectly circular in plan, nearly flat bottomed, and with convexly curved sides that tumble-home to join the stout cylindrical gunwale bounding the mouth, which is several inches less in diameter than the width at mid height. In construction a quffa is just a huge lidless basket, strengthened within by innumerable ribs radiating from around the centre of the floor. The type of basketry employed is of that widely distributed kind termed coiled basketry.' In a recent book Professor Dionysius A. Agius says: 'It consists of a spiral of reeds bundled and woven together ... The reeds are woven together with a palm fibre rope and the basket is reinforced by an inner structure. Normally two quffa-builders are needed, one for the inside, and the other for the outside, as one passes the cord through the wall of the asket while the other tightens the cord and so on'.

The size of quffas varied greatly. According to Budge Wallis, in *By Nile and Tigris 1920*, the smallest were two-seaters, whereas the largest could carry a cargo of between four and five tons, and were known to have carried three horses and several men. Passenger quffas could carry up to twenty people. Hornell states: 'Average sizes: diameter of mouth 4½ to 10 feet; depth 2½ to 4 feet'. F R Chesney (in *The Expedition for the Survey of the Rivers Euphrates and Tigris in 1835-37)* gives the smallest size as 3 feet 8 inches in diameter; the largest, 15 feet. A Baghdad informant in 1939 gave the size of the largest cargo lighters of quffa build as '16 feet 5 inches across the mouth; the maximum circumference as 57 feet, with a depth of 10 feet 6 inches. Such dimensions are wholly exceptional. A more usual size of a cargo quffa is 13 feet in mouth diameter and 7½ feet in depth.'

Fig 6 : 2
Quffa being used as a water taxi in Baghdad. Date not known.

175

Fig 6 : 3
Quffa transporting melons, possibly on the Tigris. Circa 1918.

All the British and Irish coracles are more or less the same size. Bull boats only vary as to the size of the buffalo or cowhide used to cover them. The only other coracle which varies greatly in size is the Indian coracle, which will be referred to later. The variety in size, it is suggested, is closely related to the differing uses made of the craft.

An interesting feature of quffas is mentioned by Hornell. He wrote: 'If the boatman or quffaji be superstitious, as often is the case, he will embed a few money cowries and some blue button beads in the bitumen (with which it is covered) on the outside in the hope thereby of averting the evil eye.'

Interestingly there is evidence that early in their history, quffas were covered with hide before bitumen was used. A similar progression was made by English and Welsh coracles and Donegal paddling curraghs.

Hornell records that the method of paddling varied with the size of the quffa and the number of paddles used, but in the smaller two, paddles were used; the front paddler pulling the craft and the rear paddler pushing it. Hornell, having questioned such a technique when so described by Herodotus, eventually appears to accept it as possible. It is difficult to see why he had doubts. The pulling method was used by bull boats and is still used by Donegal paddling curraghs.

Furthermore, sculling over the stern of a small boat, thus pushing it forwards, is a common practice in the United Kingdom.

Quffas were widely used as water taxis by the whole population (Fig. 6:2). More specifically, in addition to ferrying people and goods across the river they were used for bringing to market loads of melons grown on the sandbanks up stream (Fig. 6:3). They were also used as lighters for the discharge of grain cargoes brought down river by kelecks. Balfour-Paul informed the writer that he was told that quffas were used extensively in the construction of Maude bridge in Baghdad.

The quffa is a particularly important coracle-type craft, not only because of its history but because many of its features are shared by a variety of countries. Of some significance is the apparent progression in its construction from the craft described by Herodotus and that described by Hornell, but how important this is depends on how Hornell's criticism of Herodotus is considered.

Chapter Seven
THE CORACLE IN ASIA

James Hornell, writing in 1946, starts his sixth chapter thus:

> At the present day the geographical distribution of the coracle in
> Asia, although discontinuous, is spread over an extremely wide area.
> This fact suggests continuity in ancient times throughout the whole
> of the southern and central regions of that continent, a conclusion
> to which support is lent by the diversity in the form and technique
> of construction characterising the coracles of different localities ;
> divergences from the prototype are often evidence of the long lapse
> in time involved in the process of adaptation to peculiar local
> conditions and to the use of other materials than were originally
> employed.

That the distribution of coracles existed over a wide area of Asia
during the time about which Hornell was writing is indisputable.
Indeed, coracle-type craft can still be found in such diverse locations
as India, Iraq, Tibet and Vietnam today.

INDIAN CORACLES

Hornell's account headed 'Indian Coracles' is very similar to, but not
identical with, his article 'S. India: Technology' which appeared in
Man: a monthly record of Anthropological Science in 1933. They are
both based on close personal observation as well as his customarily
thorough research. This chapter attempts to bring both up to date.
Some minor difficulty was encountered over place-names etc, as he
was writing in the time of empire. His spelling will be used where I
quote from him, but modern spellings will be used when describing
what I have seen or when referring to post-independence sources.

I visited southern India in 1994. The Indian craft described will
be referred to as coracles because they fulfil the necessary criteria set
out in the introduction to this book, despite the fact that they are
called by different names locally. For instance, in the Kannada dialect
the word 'harigolu' is used, whereas in the Tamil area, the words
'paracal' or 'parisil' are used.

Hornell points out that Indian coracles are 'found in three varietal forms, characteristic of three separate areas: (a) Coimbatore and Tanjore, (b) the upper reaches of the Tunghabadra river, and (c) the lower reaches of the same river, together with some nearby stretches of the Kristna'. That being said, with one exception, their overall shape does not materially differ, but their size and methods of covering the frames do.

The exception is described by Hornell. He writes that coracles in use on the river Cauveri near Kollegal were 'quadrilateral in plan with the corners rounded.' He explained that a typical example of such a craft measured approximately 7½ feet in length; 6½ feet in width, and had a depth of 2 feet. This was in contrast to the other three types, all of which were circular in shape, having their greater width at their mouths. In this they are similar to the coracles found in Ironbridge, the Spey, certain rivers in Tibet, North America and Vietnam, but differ from those found in Wales, Iraq and other parts of Tibet.

Hornell, referring to the coracles of Coimbatore and Tanjore, states that their construction is the most simple and smallest in size; their diameters being between 5 and 6 feet. They were to be found being used on the Bhavani and upper reaches of the Cauveri rivers. He asserts that they were essentially a one-man craft, but a passenger could be carried if necessity require it. In this they were the same as British coracles. He also describes how they were used on the Pykara, a mountain stream issuing from the famous Nilgiri tea growing area famous for its trout fishing by European fly fishers.

In 1990, Joanna Bourne, a trustee of Ditchling Museum, Hassocks, in West Sussex, kindly supplied me with an extract from a book written by her mother about her life and that of her husband in India at the beginning of the twentieth century.

The following extract is headed, 'Podanur Madras Residency, S. India 1906'. She writes:

> When the Bhavani was not in flood and Jim could get away from his work, he went for some exciting expeditions in a coracle. These coracles were made of plaited reeds and looked like completely round baskets, just big enough to hold two people ... they only used one paddle. When the coracleman got to a quiet place on the river, such as a deep pool, he manoeuvred his craft to a likely spot, where

he thought the fish might be lying, so that Jim could fish that spot before being dashed through the next rapid. The coraclemen were expert fisher men themselves and spent their lives up and down the river ... getting out at the place they wanted to, carrying their coracles on their heads back to the village.

Two comments are made concerning this extract. Firstly, the reference to the coracles being made of 'strong plaited reeds' is most unusual, as the Indian coracles described by Hornell had frames made of split bamboo with a gunwale constructed of thin unsplit bamboo rods.

I saw a number of coracles in different places in India in 1994. Their construction was very similar to that described by Hornell and could not be termed as being made of 'plaited reeds'. It is difficult to see that this apparent fundamental difference of construction could be explained as an error in description, but rather suggests an unique local practice. If so, this would be a classic example of a coracle-maker using whatever materials were readily available. It will be remembered that in Chapter Two the occasional use of briars, instead of the traditional ash, on the banks of the Severn in the Shrewsbury area was attributed to the late Jack Davies.

The second point of interest is the description of how the Indian coraclemen took European fly fishermen as passengers and assisted them in locating fish. It will be recalled from Chapter Four that there was an unique practice on the river Dee at Llangollen whereby the local coraclemen travelled to and from the river on the train with their coracles so that they could transport the local riparian owners when the latter fished with rod and line.

Coracles are still being made on the Cauvery. Graham and Virginia Crerar watched Mickal Swamy Sahib, 'Fishing Boat Seller/Fish Merchant' of Hogernakal, Dharmapori, Tamil Nadu make a coracle in 1990. Subsequently they arranged for it to be transported to the National Coracle Centre in Cenarth, west Wales, where it is on view now. It is believed that it is the first Indian coracle to be shown outside India in modern times.

Hornell makes mention in *Man* of 'Tunghbadra coracles'. He describes how the coracles to found on the upper reaches of the river were lighter than those to be found on the lower reaches. He makes special reference to those which were in use at the Anagundi ferry near Hampi and the ruins of the once mighty city of Vizayanagar. He continues:

> The form is deeper than the Bhavani type, the bottom being so convex that it is definitely bowl shaped. The framework of the bottom, as at Bhavani, is open work basketry, with large hexagonal meshes, but instead of the units of each element being formed of two lengths of split bamboo, each is usually composed of three unsplit bamboos or canes laid parallel; the sides and the gunwale fascine are similar to, but stouter than the Bhavani type. An additional feature, introduced to give the greater strength needed owing to increase in dimensions, is the employment of a considerable number of curved ribs of stout unsplit bamboo crossing the interior from side to side Each is kept in place by being laced in and out of the basal basketry, the upper part towards each end is secured by a cord or hide thongs to the warp elements of the woven sides; both extremities are inserted in the angle between the marginal fascine and the inner edges of the sides. The exterior is covered with hide which is not, however, reflected over the gunwale around which pass the cords or thongs which secure the margin of the hide cover. The paddle has a fairly long handle, the blade spatulate. The ferry is maintained by a number of coracles, each between ten and eleven feet in diameter.

The following observations are made on this description. In the early part of 1994 I visited Hampi and saw coracles being used as a ferry in the manner described by Hornell. Their suitability for such use was obvious because the river is quite shallow, strewn intermittently with rocks, with not a bridge in sight. One set of coraclemen was based on one bank, with another set on the opposite side. The coracles varied considerably in size but were quite capable of carrying at least five passengers at a time. The one in which I made my first crossing was about 10' in diameter. The coracleman sat on an upturned biscuit tin and paddled with a 'C' stroke (Plate 31). His paddle was very similar to that described by Hornell. (All coracle paddles I examined in India were much heavier than the corresponding size of paddle used in Britain. It was said that they were made from palm wood.)

The coracle in which I made the return journey was smaller, but nevertheless took four people without difficulty. On this occasion the coracleman knelt close to the side of the coracle and 'scooped' with alternate hands. (The cost of a single journey was two rupees per passenger.) On land nearby there were a number of coracles of varying sizes together, with a pitch boiler and brushes for use in waterproofing the coracles, and a fishing net. I was told that these coracles were used for fishing.

Shortly before visiting Hampi I had been to a well-known dam on the Tumghabadra in the Hospet/Gunterkal area. There, some considerable distance away, I saw coracles which appeared to be similar in shape to those in use at the ferry. What was particularly interesting was the way in which they were being used. Two men were on board; one was tending a long net, whilst his companion was propelling the coracle by 'sculling' it with a large oar over the stern, in a similar manner to that used by West Country boatmen when in dinghies, tenders etc. The sculling oar was clearly secured to the coracle.

To return to the coracles seen at Hampi, none of them was covered with hide, nor, for that matter, were any of the coracles I had seen on the Cauvery. Clearly, hide had been replaced on both the Cauveri and on the upper reaches of the Tunghabadra with plastic provision sacks sewn together and made waterproof by having their outsides painted with tar – hence the pitch boiler and brushes mentioned earlier. This progression from hide to a man-made cover has taken place in England and Wales as well. In the case of British coracles, calico or canvas is much lighter as a cover than hide, and animal skins have become much more difficult to obtain. Lightness of portage would have had an attraction for the Indian coracleman, but it is by no means certain that they would have experienced the same difficulty in obtaining animal hides as their British counterparts.

Hornell does not mention how the coracles of India were carried. However, in the vicinity of Hampi an Indian coracleman was seen by me carrying his coracle on his head, without discernible strain or difficulty (Plate 32).

Hornell claims the coracles to be found on the lower reaches of the Tunghabadra near Kurnul to be the largest and finest in India, ranging from 10 feet to 14 feet in diameter, with a depth of between 3 feet and 3½ feet. He describes how they were to be found in great numbers at the Kurnul ferry; on one day, having counted thirty-six in sight from one spot. He was told that the largest was capable of transporting fifty men or forty bags of grain. It was said that a fully equipped twelve pounder gun was carried in one of these coracles.

Hornell states that the framework is more carefully constructed than either of the two earlier mentioned types. He continues: 'Instead of having but one basketwork framing, two are present – a main or inner series of stout bamboo laths, usually in threes, woven in open basketwork fashion, and an outer one of weaker laths in pairs, so arranged as to cross the larger hexagon meshes of the inner series. These coracles are punted as well as paddled. In shallow water a long bamboo quant is used but in deep water the orthodox paddle is brought into service.' In 1990 the Crerars saw large hide-covered coracles being 'punted' on the Cauveri at Trichuripall, Tamil Nadu.

Hornell further describes in detail the elaborate ceremonies which attend the launching of a new coracle at Kurnul. A somewhat muted parallel is to be found in the carrying of a bottle of holy water in a newly launched Donegal paddling curragh.

Some week after I had visited Hampi I went to Sangan on the Cauveri in the Karnataka area. Here coracles were used for leisure trips on the river and, in the early mornings, fishing. A local coracleman said (through an interpreter) that the working life of an Indian coracle was about one year. (Indeed, a number of derelict coracles were to be seen in the area.) I was also informed that the size of a coracle was dictated by local needs and nature of the river. At the same time I was told the average carrying capacity was ten persons, and that the skills required to make a coracle were passed down from father to son.

Sadly, but not surprisingly it appears that coracle-making and usage in India are now in serious decline – an all too familiar story the world over.

Mention has already been made of some of the traditional uses of coracles in India, such as ferrying and fishing, but there are others. The decline in coracle manufacture has already been mentioned, but there is a growth area and that is to be found in the field of leisure pursuits. A good example is to be found in the beautiful area of Hoggenakal Falls on the Cauveri in Tamil Nadu. Here coracles are used to take tourists to the base of the spectacular falls.

In the travel section of *The Times* of 7 January 1989, Pearson

Phillips describes travelling in coracles in Kabini, a former hunting lodge of the Maharajah of Mysore. There an irrigation dam has turned the river into a reservoir, where the coracle proves to be the ideal craft from which to observe birds and animals discreetly.

Coracles were used in May 2000 to view the Gopalkrishna temple in Mysore, then visible after fifteen years as the water level in the KR Sagar Reservoir receded.

Hornell gives examples of coracle usage. He writes 'Sir Frederick A Nicholson informs me about 40 years ago [circa 1888] road metal and other heavy goods were transported (by coracle) from the interior to the plains of Tanjore ... [also] at the beginning [of the twentieth century] some of the students attending Kumbakonan College regularly crossed the river to college in a coracle.' Most memorably, he relates, 'In the days before the Pax Brittanica suppressed internecine warfare there were infrequent requests for the purpose of transporting troops and artillery from bank to bank', and a little later mentions 'The Duke of Wellington who in his omniscient way knew and appreciated the value of these craft made use of them in his Mysore campaign in 1803'.

Fig 7 : 1
'Bowl-shaped' Tibetan coracle. (J. Hornell, 1946, plate XVI).

They were also used by imperial railway engineers whenever repairs were required to the piers of the bridge spanning the Tunghabadra near Kurnul.

Lest it be thought that these exotic uses of coracles were confined to the days of empire, the *India Express – Coimbatore,* in recent times, carried a photograph of the special task force in coracles in pursuit of a notorious criminal called Veerappam when crossing the Bhavani near Sirumugai forest.

Hornell concludes his article in *Man* thus: 'Coracles have their own special virtues for ferry purposes. They are, indeed, superior to ordinary boats. In practice a boat crosses a swift stream very obliquely, often landing a long way downstream from its point of departure; the coracle in skilled hands goes nearly straight across without great exertion on the part of the ferryman.' Anyone who has seen an Indian coracleman taking his passengers across such a river will recognise how right Hornell was when he wrote those words.

Interestingly, in eastern Bengal, in the Dacca area, the place of the coracle was taken by a craft which had much in common with the coracle. It was used in the type of area where coracles were frequently used. It was broadly circular with its rim being at the widest point, although it was hemispherical rather than having the flattened bottom possessed by most coracles. With a depth of approximately 15 inches and a diameter not exceeding 2½ feet it was clearly smaller than a coracle, but it was its composition that took it out of the classification of coracle, for it was made of earthenware. It could only function in waters where there were not any rocks. It was called a Tigari.

India is of particular interest to the student of coracles and allied craft – not only because of the numbers in use in the past and even today, but on account of the rich variety of their uses which so admirably demonstrate the versatility of the coracle.

TIBETAN CORACLES *(Called in Tibetan 'Ku-dru')*

India's neighbour, Tibet, also has a long and varied coracle tradition.

As always, it is to James Hornell's seminal work *Water Transport* that one must turn for the greatest amount of reliable information. He describes in some detail three basically different types of coracle in use in Tibet during the period he was writing about. They may be roughly categorised as follows:

1. A quadrilateral-shaped craft.
2. A bowl-shaped craft.
3. A 'food-bowl-shaped' craft (Fig. 7:1).

The first is the most well-known because it is used in the vicinity of Lhasa. Hornell quotes Hayden and Cosson's *Sport and Travel in the High Lands of Tibet* (1927) as describing it thus:

> Most are far larger than those in the eastern provinces, for traffic is far greater and often of a heavier character. The increase in size thus necessitated has caused the abandonment of the circular of bowl form and its replacement by one which is broadly oval or even sub rectangular, with length nearly double the breadth and with tumble-home sides. Considerable variation in size and shape is seen; all are very roughly constructed. The gunwales may be of several lengths of stout juniper branches with the ends overlapped and bound together, or they may be made of many slender withies lashed into a cylindrical bundle. One or two poles cross the mouth between the two long sides to act as strengthening struts. The hide is put on without any attempt at neatness, its edges looped on below the gunwales.
>
> Although the wicker framework is roughly put together, and made of a number of curved ribs transversely arranged and spaced widely apart, with a few longitudinal outer stringers crossing the ribs at right angles, it is remarkably strong and some are large enough to transport a dozen people across the strongly running river.

Hornell then gives approximate measurements and a description of the construction of one particular such coracle used by Kingdon Ward (1913) to travel fifteen miles down stream from Batang on the Chin-Sha-Chiang, a tributary of the Yangtse. 'Its length was barely 6 feet, the breadth 3 feet and the depth 5 feet. Three Yak skins, sewn together, formed the cover ... one Tibetan paddled at the fore end to ensure that the craft kept well out in the current.'

Finally, he described another voyage by Ward involving a total of five coracles down the Gyamda river. They were all apparently constructed in a similar manner to one another; each being formed of a dried Yak skin suspended from a rectangular frame to which it was bound by withies. A light framework served to keep the skin stretched. In each coracle a man sat on a cross bar in the stern, facing forwards and using a pushing stroke with a pair of pole sculls working in rawhide grommets.'

In May 1988 an article appeared in Condé Nast Traveller – New York, by Thomas Laird and Nicholas Gregory. It describes a journey they made in a Type 1 Tibetan coracle from Punt Soling to Shigatse on the river Tsangpo. They gave an interesting account of the start of their voyage thus:

> Sonam agreed to take us on the river. The following morning Sonam's donkey carried our bags down to the river, and there we found Sonam and his son spreading out the Yak skins, wooden poles, and juniper branches. The skins had been soaked the entire previous night and were now soft and supple. It took only 2 hours for Sonam and his son to lay them out, fit the poles into place, lash fresh branches to their ends, and then snugly bow them upward to form the sides of a 3 foot deep, flat bottomed shell of stretched Yak skin.
>
> Sonam said that the villages up river from Shigastse used the Tsangpo to deliver firewood and other items to the Shigastse market. Soon, he thought, the traffic would cease because so many roads were being built. Within 5 or 10 years, if he is right, the last coracle will float down the Tsangpo and out of the history of man.
>
> By noon Sonam's coracle was ready. It was light enough for him to carry to the river. Using a Yak-wool rope, he slowly lowered it down to the surface of the water. We helped Sonam to load the firewood and our baggage into the coracle, then took our places atop the wood.'

Interestingly, they mentioned that if they had not had the ballast-like qualities of the firewood they would have overturned.

This is an example of the fact that a heavily-laden coracle is generally more stable than a lighter one.

Subsequent to reading this article, I corresponded with Thomas Laird in July 1988. Laird said that Tibetans think nothing of taking their coracles apart and loading them on donkeys, and then reassembling them later if required.

He also informed me that: 'Tibetans appear to make several types of coracles some larger and some smaller. Also they appear to construct ones intended to be left assembled for long periods of time and ones that will remain assembled for only a week or so before being taken apart and dried out for long term storage.'

It will be remembered that in Chapter Six, when referring to the quffas of Iraq, a challenge was made to the validity of Hornell's criticism of Herodotus' description of crafts being dismantled at the end of a journey. The above described Tibetan practice would appear to support Herodotus' view rather than that of Hornell.

In the November/December 1989 edition of *Classic Boat,* Sarah Locke, the international photographer and journalist (known to me since her childhood) wrote an article dealing exclusively with Tibetan coracles in general and Type One coracles in particular. She drew attention to the longevity of skin boats in Tibet 'which are mentioned in China's historical literature as early as in the fourth century.' She cited their importance as ferries in support of this, specifically mentioning their use as ferries to cross the Kyichu river in Lhasa, and went on to say, 'It would have been at this point that the Dalai Lama and his entourage crossed in coracles as they fled from the Chinese occupation in 1959 en route to India.'.

She also mentioned the use of coracles for fishing.

Her description of the construction of the quadrilateral coracle was much simpler than that of Hornell. She wrote:

> Four branches are lashed together with a rope made of yak hair to form a rectangle which is narrower at one end, the bow. A light frame of willow is then strung from this rectangle to form the distinctive coracle shape. The yak hide is stretched across this frame and attached to the rectangular structure by rope. The boats are flat bottomed and passengers must place their weight on the frame, not on the skin ... the size of the coracle varies from 6 feet with a width of 3 feet at the bow and 4 feet at the stern, to as large as 10 feet long with a width of 4 feet 6 inches at the bow and 6 feet at the stern.

She pointed out that the coracle is only used for downstream journeys. To return, the coracle is carried by the coracleman or by a goat. Her description of how these craft are propelled is basically the same as that of Hornell so far as the use of oars is concerned, and they agreed that the coracleman sits at one end of the craft; Sarah Locke, however, said it was the bow, i.e. the narrower end, whereas Hornell claims it to be the stern. It is feared that Sarah fell into the common trap of thinking that the narrower end of a coracle is its bow, whereas in practice it is the broader end. Be that as it may, they both agreed that the vessel is propelled by being pushed rather than pulled.

Sarah Locke reported that when the coracle was carried over land a piece of wood or a rope was secured to the gunwale. The use of this aid enabled the coracleman to carry a craft much longer than he is tall. Another interesting observation she made related to the carriage of goods by coracle. In those circumstances logs were laid across the gunwale and the items to be carried piled onto them, rather than being put into the coracle itself.

She also described how fishing is carried out by Tibetan coracles. She wrote:

> The coracles are also used for fishing which takes place only in the later afternoon and evening. Two people are needed; one afloat and one ashore. One end of a net, made of yak hair, is tied to a rock on the bank and then let out gradually whilst the coracle is propelled across the river by rowing and down stream by the current. The boat then returns to the original bank and the net is gathered in whilst the boatman carries his boat back along the bank upstream.

Hornell's second category is now considered. Of all the types of Tibetan coracle he states that this is the smallest and also the simplest. It was found to be in use on the river Yangtse. No photograph, drawing or sketch of one is available but Hornell describes it as follows: 'it is ... a wide mouthed shallow bowl made of Yak hide stretched over a wide meshed framework of juniper branches. Outwardly it is almost identical with the coracles in use on the hill streams of the Nilgiri hills in south India, but the construction of the frame work is less elaborate; the ribs here are in two series only, widely spaced, crossing at right angles to one another, thereby forming square meshes instead of hexagonal ones. The edge of the covering hide is reflected over the cylindrical gunwales, composed of several long withies bound together.'

Apparently they held between two and four people, and were used at the Ganto and Rushi Drango ferries in eastern Tibet, close to the Chinese border.

Elizabeth B Booz, in *A Guide to Tibet* (1986), writing about the Yarlong Tsangpo river, states: 'along the 650 km (400 miles) of its middle reaches, a wide, navigable channel, shifting with the seasons, is plied by … *round* coracles made of Yak hide and willow boughs.' This might well be the modern version of the craft mentioned above by Hornell.

The final type of coracle described by Hornell in many ways is the most interesting. It could be argued that the 'quadrilateral' coracle is not a coracle, because it is propelled by oars, but it has been included because there is at least one reference to its being controlled by a single paddle; it may well be that its oars are a later edition to supplement a single paddle rather than to supplant it, in the same way that the Donegal paddling curragh evolved. It could be that a single paddle would have been used when fishing, rather than when it was used for the carriage of people or cargo. On balance, however, I am inclined to think it is, and always has been, propelled by two oars and not a single paddle.

Hornell's is the only description of the third type of Tibetan coracle but, fortunately, there is a photograph which clearly shows what it looks like. It can be found in his book, *Water Transport.*

These coracles were to be found on the river Yalung, flowing parallel to and eastward of the Upper Yangtse. Mrs Louis King (Rin-Chen-Lha Moi), referred to by Hornell describes it in this way:

> … the sides narrowing toward the mouth, a shape resembling that of the food bowl carried by every Tibetan. This similarity is eluded to in the common Tibetan jibe that likens the dimensions of the oversize bowl of the greedy eater to those of a coracle.
>
> These Yalung coracles, about 6 feet in greatest diameter have the hide covering of the flattened bottom made from a circular disc cut from a large hide, the sides are usually of two pieces sewn together at both ends and along the lower edge to the margin of the bottom disc. The seam thus formed around the bottom is prominent and characteristic, forming as it were a circumferential bilge which may have some slight value in steadying the craft. The gunwale as usual is made up of numerous thin juniper withies bound together; the margin of the cover, which is not reflected over it, is laced on carefully around its lower edge by many thong loops.
>
> One of these coracles can carry from three to five people and is light enough to be carried on a man's back. The paddle is short handled with a long shouldered blade, fairly long and parallel sided.

A further insight into Tibetan coracles generally is to be found in

Tibet Past and Present (1925), by Sir Charles Bell, who wrote:

> The boats or coracles are made from the hide of yaks and other cattle, stretched on the framework of withies. These latter are sometimes of willow, but preferably sliced from the tougher wood of the thorny scrub, known in Lahsa as 'LA', which grows in profusion along the river banks in the uplands of central Tibet. Often do we see the Tibetan boatman, carrying his coracle 10 or 12 miles a day upstream, accompanied by a solitary sheep, which carries his food and other necessaries.
>
> Fragile as they seem, for the task before them and, when empty, drawing only a few inches of water it is nevertheless remarkable what these coracles will carry. At Shigatse I have seen a large family in its little hide coat – as the Tibetans call them – after their donkey has clambered beside them, paddle across the broad river to its northern bank and down the river that flows by Lhasa, a river as broad as the Thames and twice as long – one may seen daily a succession of these coracles carrying not only loads of passengers and light goods but long heavy logs of poplar and walnut.'

The inevitable conclusion which must be drawn from the above is that the coracle in times gone by stretched into every corner of Tibetan life, and to a lesser extent still does today.

THE TUB BOATS OF CHINA AND JAPAN

Neither the Chinese nor the Japanese have coracles or any form of skin boats, but they do have tub boats. They are tubs built of short wooden staves, barrel fashioned, bound round with iron hoops. A typical craft would be about 7' to 8' long, by about 4½' wide and 2' deep. They are paddled on each side with two short-handled paddles. They were to be found in Fujian province towards the end of the twentieth century.

MONGOLIAN CORACLES

There is but one reference to the existence of coracles in Mongolia. Hornell refers to there having been coracles in 'the extreme south of Mongolia', but does not provide any information about them.

VIETNAMESE CORACLES *(THUNG CHAI)*

This chapter is concluded by considering coracles which were and are to be found in Vietnam (Plate 33). If reliance was put solely on written contributions about these craft it would not be appreciated quite how important they actually are to the study of coracles and their allied craft.

In *Boats of the World*, McGrail states, 'No example [he is referring to the wider category of basket boats in Vietnam which, of course, includes coracles] has been excavated, and there is no other documentation before the early 19th century reports, nevertheless, the materials tools and techniques needed to build them are such that much earlier use is likely.'

Having recently seen coracles being made and used in Vietnam, and having spoken to their makers and users, I agree with this opinion.

In 1969, Robert F. Cairo observed woven basket boats in the watered areas of Da Nang. This, together with 'a modicum of information from published sources' formed the basis of an article by him entitled 'A Note on South Vietnamese Basket Boats', which will be referred to at greater length later. He started his article by saying, 'In much of South Vietnam, if one finds a body of water, he is likely to find basket boats on it.' This was still as true in 2001 as it was then (Plate 34).

From personal observation in 2001, I confidently assert that there is nowhere in the world where one can see more coracles than in Vietnam, nor where they play a greater part in local life in, or near to, the central areas of this part of the Far East.

Listed below, in chronological order, are publications which refer to coracles but, in many cases, are primarily concerned with Vietnamese basket boats generally.

Voileurs d'Indochine, Sili-Saigon, J. B. Pietri.
Cairo regards this as an important source of material on boats of Indo-China, and particularly refers to Pietri's account of the composition of caulking. This will be returned to later when it is considered how Vietnamese coracles were and are made waterproof.

A Study of Ancient Ships of Japan, Part IV: 'Skin Boats', Nishmura - Tokyo Society of Naval Architects (1931)
Hornell refers in general terms to the basket boats of Tongking. It is obvious from the line drawings of the craft he was considering that it is not a coracle but a small oared craft, similar in technique of construction to a coracle but not in shape or function. These craft which, apparently, do not have a specific name are found much more widely than coracles. The only relevance of Hornell's contribution is again in relation to caulking. When discussing this he relies wholly on this book.

It is very surprising indeed that Hornell makes no mention of Vietnamese coracles having regard both to their numbers and the substantial part they play in local coastal life.

Bois et Bateau du Vietnam F Aubaille-Salenave, Paris SELAF Ethnosciences, No 3, 1987
This book includes a line drawing of a central Vietnamese coracle and later a photograph of two craft, more oval in shape, than the majority of coracles. They show women using them for gathering vegetables in North Vietnam. But the author does not make a specific reference to coracles as such.

Notes on the Watercraft of Thanh Hoa province, North Vietnam, The International Journal of Nautical Archeology, 1994 23.3 229-238
Nick Burmingham of the Western Australia Maritime Museum, Freemantle, Australia, describes collecting data during the months December 1992-April 1993, mainly in Sam Son in Than Hoa and Quang Ninh province, concerning three types of traditional watercraft. Once again the craft in question appeared to be constructed in the similar way to coracles but are essentially different in shape and method of propulsion. They cannot be classified as coracles, being clearly 'boat-shaped' and propelled either by oars or engine. Additionally, it should be noted that the weave used in their construction is not the same as that used in coracles.

Most relevant of all the books, articles, etc which have been referred to so far is that of Robert Cairo. He wrote his note to fill a gap as, in his opinion, so little had been written about Vietnamese coracles. Whilst he wrote generally about basket boats, he is the only person to have written in any detail about Vietnamese coracles which he aptly refers to as 'bamboo coracles'. The first point that he makes is that 'published sources have little to say about Vietnamese coracles'. Several of his observations are borne out by what I saw in Da Nang in 2002.

In particular, Cairo mentions the following:

1. The coracles are ubiquitous.
2. Virtually all fishing boats carry coracles if they are large enough to do so.
3. That they operate on occasions as far as two miles from the coast.
4. They are used by net handlers, fishermen and as tenders.
5. The smallest coracles have little or no interior framing.

Interestingly, he saw some coracles which 'employed a sail of the standing or working lug type.'

Amongst the hundreds of coracles I saw, none used a sail, nor did they appear to have the wherewithal to step a mast. Having said this there is no reason to doubt what Cairo saw, but, perhaps, the engine has largely replaced sail in central Vietnam as elsewhere in the world.

I have to differ with Cairo concerning the use of engines in coracles. I saw coracles with inboard engines on a number of occasions. Plate 35, a photograph I took in the Da Nang area in 2001, is a good example.

Cairo asserts that 'Rattan is generally used as a lashing material but I have seen wire employed'. Local coracle-makers confirmed to me that rattan was used in the past as a lashing but nowadays nylon line is used. This was witnessed on several occasions. It would appear to be the sole constructional development since the time Cairo wrote about. He had noted that rattan was beginning to be replaced by wire, and it clearly has now been superseded by nylon line.

The methods of construction (as opposed to materials) and propulsion he described differ not at all from modern practices.

Interestingly, Robert Cairo's comments concerning the materials used for caulking are derived from the writings of Nishimura and in *Esquise d'une ethnographie naviale des peoples annamites* by P. Paris (1955), which are largely in accord with current practices whereby the frame is made waterproof by an application of ox dung, which is later coated with resin from the raie tree.

He lists other recipes for caulking as follows:

1. Ground bamboo and resin.[1]
2. Mangrove bark, coconut bark, bamboo strips, Tram tree skin and cocoa husk fibres.
3. Resin substance made of pitch obtained from pine trees and mixed with ground bamboo or sea shells.[2]

At no stage does it appear that Cairo enquired as to the prevalent caulking practices when he was in the Da Nang area of Vietnam in 1969. The question of caulking will be returned to later but, suffice it to say, that not one of the four coracle-makers I interviewed had ever heard of the ingredients mixed with resin other than ox dung, despite the fact that some of them were old enough to have heard of such earlier practices but had not done so.

The most recent description of Vietnamese coracles is to be found in *Boats of the World*, by Professor Sean McGrail. What has been written in it is not disputed, except in relation to the description of rattan strips being used contemporarily to lash the gunwhale and bamboo mat together which has now been superseded by nylon line as mentioned earlier. Also issue is taken with Professor McGrail over the ingredients of the caulking mixture he mentions. Dung and resin are regularly used, but I did not discover any evidence of use of the other materials to which McGrail refers. As McGrail was writing exclusively about basket boats generally, it is not always easy to tell when he is discussing coracles or other types of basket boats.

Moreover, McGrail states that 'It is then further supported by bamboo framing timbers.' I observed that while some coracles had such supports, others had none at all. The rule appeared to be the larger the coracle the greater the number of supporting laths, as Plate 36 demonstrates.

The editor of the Coracle Society's newsletter travelled extensively in Vietnam in 2000. Whilst there he sought out coracles and spoke to local tour guides throughout the country.

He was told that coracles were only to be found in central Vietnam. (My observations and discussions whilst in Vietnam were to the same effect.) He saw hundreds of coracles in the areas of Da Nang, Hoi An and Cham island (Culao Cham) and has seen photographs of many coracles in Nha Trang.

La Van Tien, the first coracle-maker I interviewed on 23 April 2001 in Than Khe, told me that he had received orders to make coracles for people from Hue (north of Da Nang) Quang Tri (north of Hue) and Quang Dien (between Hue and Quang Tri).

Additionally two books provide pictorial evidence of coracles elsewhere in Vietnam. In *Vietnam*, by Hans Kemp, is a photograph of two girls en route to the market in Phu Quoc which is south west of Ho Chi Minh City, and another photograph of a family in a coracle, also at Phu Quoc. In *Our World in Colour* (Vietnam Guide Book Company), there are two photographs of coracles in Vung Tua, 128 km east of Hoi Chi Minh City.

From the above it would appear that whilst the majority of coracles are to be found in central Vietnam, a limited number can be found in the north and south of the country.

In the spring of 2001 I interviewed four coracle-makers, namely La Van Thien of Than Ke near Da Nang, Phan Tri and Phan Dung in Thoquang also near Da Nang, Do Kha of Cam Kim Island near Hoi An, and Tran Sang of Duy Binh village, also near Hoi An. From them, I understood that coracles varied greatly in size, the smallest being 1.2 metres in diameter and the largest 3 metres. (The largest of the coracles frequently had engines.) La Van Thien told me that he made five sizes of coracles, all reducing from 2.4 metres in diameter by 20 cm. The largest of the coracles made by Phan Tri and Phan Dung were oval in shape and measured 4.5 metres by 3 metres by 72 cm. These were exceptional in shape, as all the other coracles made by these coracle-makers were invariably circular in shape.

My observation of the many coracles I saw in Vietnam was that they were circular crafts in the main. Their depth varied upwards from half a metre, depending on their overall size. What I saw in Vietnam bore out what I was told by the coracle-makers so far as size and shape were concerned.

A distinguishing feature of these coracles is to be found in their paddles. Whilst they varied greatly in size depending on the overall size of the coracle, they were all very long by European, Indian or Native American standards. A coracle which was made in Vietnam in

2001 for me measures 1.5 metres in diameter but has a paddle measuring 183 cm in length. This is not unusual. It is suggested there are two reasons for this unusual length. Firstly, coracles are frequently paddled with the coracleman adopting a standing position and, secondly, a long paddle is useful as a makeshift punt pole in shallow coastal waters where the majority of coracles are to be found.

All British coracle paddles have either a 'T-bar' (e.g Ironbridge coracles) or 'no T-bar' (e.g Tywi coracles), but in Vietnam there is a mixture of both types. It is suggested that this is due to the rich variety of usage of these coracles.

Cairo mentioned that coracles were used in Vietnam by net handlers for fishing boats, individual fishermen and for support (while in Vietnam I either saw or was told of such usage), but he did not see coracles used for gathering vegetables as described by Aubaille-Sallenave, but whilst en route to Duy Binh Village two small coracles were observed by me which were being used to spray fumigants on maize crops.

One of the most common uses is undoubtedly to assist in setting fishing nets at sea, and that is why many coracles are carried by larger fishing boats (Plate 37). Coracles are also used for individual net fishing.

Flooding is a recurrent danger in the islands and costal areas of Hoi An. This is particularly so in Cam Kin Island. I was told by Dho Kha that many people had coracles for flood evacuation purposes. Tran Sang also said that everyone in his village had a coracle 'to escape the ravages of the annual floods.'

I learnt of a very unusual use for coracles from my interpreter, Tu Van Dung. Apparently, during the war with the Americans, the Viet Cong used coracles for surveillance purposes in the paddy fields and along the rivers in the Da Nang region. He had been told of this by an American veteran who had first-hand experience whilst serving in Vietnam.

The sheer number of coracles to be found in every coastal village of central Vietnam, together with what has already been written in this chapter, show what a crucial role the coracle plays in local life in coastal Vietnam. It is infinitely greater than anything which can be found in any other country.

It is significant that during the whole time I was in Vietnam I never saw an inflatable or similar craft, every craft of a similar nature being made of bamboo.

Out of the coracle-makers I interviewed, three confirmed that coracle manufacture was increasing. The reasons put forward to explain this state of affairs were as follows:

Than Khe: 'More people are fishing; fishing boats are increasing in size as a result of modern technology and the government has permitted an increase in local fishing areas.'

Phan Tri and Phan Dung: 'More people are working on fishing boats which are increasing in size, and the government has invested more money in the area which had led to an increase in fishing.'

Tran Sang: 'A fishing career has become more professional nowadays, and this has led to an increase in the number of people fishing.'

Do Kha, the dissenting voice, however, said that whereas some years ago there were other coracle-makers in his village, now he is the only one. He attributed this decline to the work being too hard and villagers preferring to do other, easier, work which was now available. His assessment of the current situation is what one would find in India, Tibet and Iraq, to say nothing of Britain and Ireland, but overall, the coracle tradition in Vietnam is thriving. This is borne out by the fact that all four coracle-makers work full-time in their trade, a situation not encountered elsewhere.

The construction of Vietnamese coracles will now be considered. There was considerable similarity of constructional techniques amongst those whom I witnessed making coracles, although some variation in the tools used occurred. All, at some stage in the process, used the same long knife (called 'mak' in the Da Nang area) which was invariably made by the local blacksmith. One was brought back and given to the National Coracle Centre at Cenarth Falls in west Wales. Only one of the coracle-makers used a tool similar to a billhook for splitting the bamboo before cleaving it, the others using the mak. All used clamps to hold together the gunwale and the bamboo mat which formed the hull of the coracle. Two used large conventional adjustable metal clamps, but the other two used a primitive form of wooden clamp which resembled a large clothes peg. After it had been placed over the gunwale and mat it was tightened by a large wooden wedge hammered into its top. When this had been done, the gunwale and mat was secured with nylon line. One of these tools was also brought back from Vietnam and given to the National Coracle Centre.

One of the coracle-makers used a bow saw for cutting the bamboo poles to the required length. Another used a chisel to trim the protruding edges of the mat. Other tools used were a wooden mallet to knock the mat into shape, the metal fid to pierce the mat to enable the nylon ties to be inserted, and a piece of bamboo was worn on the finger of one coracle-maker to protect him when cleaving the bamboo into thin pieces.

All the coracle-makers bought their bamboo from a middle man. The bamboo varied in age from between two and seven years old. The older bamboo was soaked before being used to make it more pliable. In one case soaking took place irrespective of age as a precaution against termites.

First of all a quantity of bamboo was cut into strips about one inch in width. Poles were then driven into the ground to provide a circular shape, and a gunwale consisting of two overlapping semicircles of split slender bamboo poles was tied to the inside of the gunwale (Plate 38).

The mat was then woven. It had two different types of weave which enabled it to be forced subsequently into the required shape (Plate 39). The mat, having been placed on the gunwale, was then forced down by the coracle-maker standing on it. Having done this, he sat down inside the mat hull and kicked it into a perfect shape with his bare feet, remarkably achieving a completely smooth shape without any tucks or creases (Plate 40). Then the mat hull was pierced by a fid and secured to the gunwale at four equidistant points with thin bamboo strips (Plate 41). This was followed by the addition of a second gunwale on the inside of the hull, any protruding parts of the hull being trimmed to give a smooth finish (Plate 51). Finally the two gunwales and the hull, having been clamped, were lashed together with nylon line.

Except in the case of the smaller coracles, strengthening bamboo laths were added internally. (Out of the very many coracles I saw, only one had protecting laths on the outside of its hull, presumably for protective purposes when, perhaps, it had to be dragged over rough ground or shingle.)

To make the coracle watertight, ox dung was mixed with water and the hull coated with it. After it had dried, the resin from the 'rai' tree was boiled and spread over it. This technique was invariably used in the coastal areas of central Vietnam, although very occasionally coracles were seen with what appeared to be a coating of bitumen. These appeared to be older craft in need, no doubt, of later maintenance.

Paddles were made of a wood called locally 'Kien Kien', which had the hardness of teak.

Vietnamese coracles are propelled in a number of different ways. Sometimes the paddlers stand whilst paddling, on other occasions they kneel, less frequently they sit. On occasions a 'figure of eight' or a 'C' stroke are used, as with British coracles. Also a 'scooping' stroke similar to that utilised by Native American bull boat handlers is used.

It is not unusual to see two people sitting or kneeling side by side and paddling over each side. More unusually, but not infrequently, a particularly long paddle with a 'T-bar' is lashed to the gunwale. The coracle is then moved forward at considerable speed by short sharp alternative twists of the T-bar and a rocking motion of the paddle.

Finally, Cairo describes a very unusual technique. He writes: 'the boatman using a technique of weight shifting, rocking or bouncing if you will, and it is surprising just how well they do in a ground swell. By a co-ordinated movement of arms, trunk and legs, the centre of gravity is shifted (or rocked ahead a bit at a time) and this force tends to slide the boat forward'.

Thanks to the generosity of a traditional coracle enthusiast, Paul W Jones of Newcastle under Lyne, Staffs, I was able to view a DVD which showed coracle racing in Vietnam in the 1950s. Some of the scenes would be familiar to anyone who had witnessed coracle races in Wales or England: the paddle strokes employed were identical, as was the level of skill displayed, but what distinguished races in Vietnam from those in Great Britain was a particular race where the participants employed the very technique described by Cairo to which reference has just been made. What particularly impressed was the speed generated by this technique! There can be little doubt that the 'bowl shape' of the Vietnamese coracle greatly assisted this variant of the coracle races.

To this list must be added the use of engines and sails, to which reference has already been made.

It will be apparent that the Vietnamese coracle has been considered at considerably greater length than any other individual type of coracle. This is for two different but equally important reasons: firstly, the Vietnamese coracle, because of its numbers, variety, sophisticated construction, and social importance, makes it probably one of the most important of all coracles in the world; secondly, there is so little that has been written about them.

Notes

[1] *The Blue Book of Coastal Vessels, South Vietnam* (Columbus, Ohio: Remote Area Conflict Information Center, 1967), referred to in *Notes on the Watercraft of Than Hoi Province, N. Vietnam*, Nick Burningham, reported in the International Journal of Nautical Archaeology, 1994, 23.3:229-238.

[2] *The Junk Blue Book: A Handbook of Junks of South Vietnam* (Washington DC : Advances Research Projects Agency DOD, 1962).

AFTERWORD

I have pondered long and hard why coracles and their allied craft should have fascinated me for so many years. I have come to the conclusion that it is because of their immensely long and uninterrupted history, their rich diversity, and the comparative ease with which they can be made and used today.

Hornell states:

> The original home of skin boats would appear to be in Asia, for there we find them most widely distributed and boasting an ancestry traceable in history and sculptured record in a time early in the first millennium BC ... here we have one of the earliest inventions made by man in his attempt to harness the rivers of his homeland to his needs and thereby to lessen the difficulties of travel and transport.

In my humble opinion this measured statement cannot be improved upon.

Furthermore, Hornell asserts that the coracles of Asia are the progenitors of those found in Europe and America because Asian coracles were spread over such a wide area and are diverse in form and technique of construction. So far as Great Britain and Ireland are concerned it is difficult to accept that their origins can be traced back to early times in Asia. I would suggest it is far more likely that they originated spontaneously to meet the particular needs of their localities. Support for this proposition can be found in a study of the evolution of coracles and allied craft.

If one starts with Native American bull boats as the most likely model of the early coracle, it will be seen that early changes in constructional techniques are discernible. For example, the 'Older Dakota Boat' has laths which appear to have been cleaved (a slightly more sophisticated process than the whole laths found in other bull boats). Again it will be recalled that there is anecdotal evidence of coracles used on the Montana Reservation with a cover made of paper impregnated with shellac.

There are many examples of evolution in British coracles. Hide was the universal covering, to be followed by flannel in Wales, which, in turn, was replaced by calico, canvas, and even denim.

The earliest form of whole green poles gave way to cleft wood and later was followed in very rare cases by zinc, and, less rarely, by aluminium, until the entire hull was, on occasions, made of fibre glass.

It will be remembered that the coracle's carrying strap originally consisted of twisted hazel or willow, followed by leather and rope, and, ultimately in Teifi coracles, by electric cabling.

The Teifi coracle has for many years been constructed as it is today, although there is some evidence that the earliest coracles to be found on the river Teifi were roughly circular. Their sister craft on the Tywi, whilst maintaining their basic shape, exhibited changes to their gunwale construction. The traditional construction of twisted hazel wands gave way to a sawn ash gunwale. The nearby Taf river coracle originally had a gunwale made of split applewood. The late Edgeworth Evans, however, used a coracle which was very similar to Tywi coracles, and which had an ash plank gunwale.

The evolutionary process is clearly shown in the principal uses of coracles. The first of these was the transporting of people and objects, by Native Americans. Coracles were adapted for fishing with nets in Wales only at the beginning of the nineteenth century.

Coracle construction in some areas was much more sophisticated than in others. Good examples are to be round in Vietnam and India, the Dwyryd coracles in Wales, and the Shrewsbury coracle kept in the Museum of Welsh Life in Cardiff (which was made by H. Hudson). Also the 'Stanley' Bewdley coracle is of a sophisticated construction.

Finally, there is clear evidence of evolution in coracles found in Asia. The original coverings of Indian coracles consisted of animal hides, but are now made of plastic provision bags which are sewn together and made waterproof by being painted with tar. Robert Cairo records seeing Vietnamese coracles under sail in the 1960s. In recent times, however, I didn't see any coracles under sail, but I did see large Vietnamese coracles to which motors were attached.

To me, the saddest aspect of coracles is that they are almost universally in decline.

Coracles and allied craft belong to the same family which has a rich diversity in their construction and usage, and which are still to be found over a large part of the world. Today their greatest density is in Asia, but within recent recorded memory huge numbers of coracles were used in Great Britain and Ireland. Sadly, everywhere they are in serious decline – except in Vietnam.

For example, Britain coracles were encountered in great numbers, particularly along the Severn (in Welshpool, Shrewsbury, Ironbridge, Bridgnorth and Bewdley), and on the Avon. They might also have been seen on the Thames and near Tewkesbury on the Severn. In Scotland, they were encountered on the Spey and possibly in other parts of the country. In Ireland, paddling coracles are still made and used in the Donegal area. Moreover, coracles existed on the Boyne in 1948, and throughout Ireland before that.

But it is in Wales where the density of coracles was most high. Today it is only on the Teifi, the Taf and the Tywi that coracles are used in the traditional way. In the 1920s and 1930s they were to be found in use on the lower Dee and Eastern Cleddau. In passing, it should be observed that coracles were in use on the upper Dee as relatively recently as the late 1940s. In the nineteenth century other rivers such as the Wye, Usk, Monnow, Conwy, Dyfi, Nevern, Llugwy, Taff, Cothi and Llwchwr were fished with coracles. When a comparison is made of current coracle usage and that which occurred in the past, the extent of the decline in coracle usage is readily apparent.

Before considering the reasons for this decline in coracle usage, it should be pointed out that there are a number of apparent anomalies.

For instance, why did the Spey curragh cease to exist very many years ago, the Boyne curragh until 1948, whereas the Donegal paddling curragh continues to this day?

And why are the number of licenses and fees charged on the Teifi and Tywi different?

Also, why are coracles in India in decline, but thriving in Vietnam?

And on a more practical note, why was animal hide used as a cover for Bewdley coracles so many years after it ceased to be used as a cover on other English coracles?

It is submitted that the reasons for decline are many and varied.

Some are physical in nature, such as the provision of roads and bridges where formerly they did not exist. An example of the former is to be found in Tibet as it modernises, and of the latter on the Severn, where new bridges were added to the famous Iron Bridge.

The rise in river pollution levels from nearby mines, as on the Llwchwr and the Dyfi, was a significant factor in reduced fish stocks.

Additionally, as the standard of living increased in an area, then poaching with a coracle was no longer necessary to feed the coracleman's family and friends.

Of current significance is the decrease in the numbers of salmon and sea trout in the rivers of west Wales, particularly at a time when net license fees have increased so substantially.

Personal factors have played their part, as when the last traditional coracleman on the upper Dee at Llangollen died shortly after the end of the last war. And the death of Eustace Rogers brought to an end his family's centuries-old coracle tradition in Ironbridge.

Finally, mention must be made of the disturbing decision by the Authorities not only to decrease the number of net licences on the Tywi at a time when fish stocks were low and licence fees, in the opinion of many, unreasonably high.

The coracle net-fishermen have responded with understandable anger to the argument advanced for this conduct: i.e, that it is in order to conserve fish stocks. The netsmen argue that they are already severely restructed as to the days and times during which they are allowed to fish, and that their nets are specifically constructed so as to avoid over-fishing. They also put forward the fact that their age-old voluntary practices are designed to keep fish stocks at sensible levels.

They feel that it was grossly unfair that the appropriate Net Limitation Order reducing the licenses from twelve to eight was brough into effect without any adequate consultation with them.

Finally on this issue: the Tywi net fishermen believe it is most unjust that the Tywi net-fishermen should have been treated in this way when anglers, who take many more fish from the river than the coracle fishermen, are not treated in a similar way, and when no apparent regard has been given to the depredations of fish stocks by the rapidly spiralling increase in seals in British rivers and coastal waters. This problem was graphically described in an article which appeared in the *Yorkshire Post* on 5 April 2008, in which it was stated:

> there is evidence that seals are more desperate for food – raiding those that are netted, pursuing salmon and sea trout through the estuaries into the rivers. Our most precious fish is the salmon. The Atlantic salmon are in decline, and they are more vulnerable to attack from seals.

It is significant that in the one country where coracles are not in decline – Vietnam – it is because the national government, according to the traditional coracle-makers, support and encourage the fishing industry.

Having regard to the fact that coracles are a fundamental part of the heritage of Wales, it is incumbent on the Government, and particularly the Welsh Assembly, to encourage and protect those who make and use coracles in the traditional way, rather than penalising them with high fees and wholly unreasonable reduction in licence numbers.

In the long history of Great Britain, as has been mentioned, coracles could be found in considerable numbers, but now they are confined to following their traditional way of life on – at most – three rivers.

If steps are not taken urgently this unique aspect of Welsh rural culture will be lost for ever. Happily it seems there are encouraging signs of change in the attitude of the Authorities.

Following representations by me, on behalf of the Coracle Society, to the Welsh Assembly, I was informed, in a letter of 20 October 2008, that the Minister for Rural Affairs takes the issue of preserving heritage fisheries very seriously and fully recognises their importance to Wales. Furthermore, she has agreed to review the current Net Limitation Order after five years, as opposed to the usual ten years. Most importantly, in the same letter, it is stated that '... the Minister has suggested the introduction of '... heritage licences, which could be issued for training other fishermen or for the use in public displays. These licenses would ensure the survival of the coracle heritage fishery.'

On a more encouraging note, it should not be overlooked that thanks to the pioneering courses in coracle construction which took place in the Greenwood Centre in Shropshire (formerly led by Gerwyn Lewis and now by Terry Kenny), and Bewdley Museum (led by Charles Fogg), together with the emergence of the Coracle Society of England and Wales, there has been a resurgence of making and use of coracles for leisure purposes. This welcome activity is now also to be found in the area of the river Boyne in Ireland.

Such encouragement, together with the fact that coracles are light enough to be transported and paddled by a single person, and some types are relatively easy to construct, has enabled a considerable number of people to enjoy the delights of our rivers. Most significantly, it has also led to a greater appreciation of these unique and historically important craft.

However, very welcome as this all is, it is no substitute for the pro-active maintenance of a traditional way of life which predates Christianity.

APPENDIX

Dimensions of lower Dee and upper Dee coracles

Lower Dee coracles: Dimensions
Length overall: 4' 7"
Greatest beam of four compartment at gunwale level: 3' 2"
At bilge: 3' 11"
At seat, inside: 35"
Length of seat: 38"
Width: 11"
Thickness: ½"
Depth to top of gunwale: 14"
Laths of ash: ¾" wide by ⅙" thick.

Weight of coracle when new: 25 lbs

Upper Dee Coracles: Dimensions
The dimensions of the ash- and aluminium-framed coracles agree
very closely. They are as follows:

	Ash-framed		Aluminium-framed	
	ft	ins	ft	ins
Length overall	4	9	4	9½
Length from fore end to seat	2	3	2	4
Length from seat to stern	1	7	1	7
Width of seat		11		10½
Length of seat	3	½	3	3½
Beam of gunwale amidships	3	2	3	2
Beam of bilge, outside	4	5	4	7
Greatest beam of fore compartment				
at gunwale	3	3	3	5
Depth at seat	1	2	1	2
Height at each end	1	8	1	7½
Height amidships	1	5	1	5
Weight	About 50 lbs		40 – 50 lbs	

The aluminium laths are 1½" wide by ¹⁄₁₆" thick.

Sources Used

Author's personal archive: various letters and documents.

'The Coracles of the Tigris & the Euphrates' in *MM* (1938)
Cairo F, 'Notes on S. Vietnam Boats' in *MM* (1972)

Bewdley Museum Article, author unknown (circa 1880)
'Green Mounds for Redskins', Christian Science Monitor (1939)
Date unknown Rogers B. Saga Magazine (date unknown)

Hudson, Marilyn, Curator, Three Tribes Museum, N orth Dakota , U.S.A. 'Sgt Pryor's Failed Ride' Information Sheet (1999)

Adney, Edwin Tappar, and Chappelle, Howard, *The Bark Canoes and Skin Boats of North America* (Washington DC 1983)
Agius, Dionysius A., *Classic Ships of Islam from Mesopotamia and the Indian Ocean* (2008)
Ahler, Stanley A et al, *People of the Willows* (1991)
Aubaille-Sallenave, F, *Bois du Vietnam* (Paris Selaf Ethnosciences 3, 1987)
Aubrey, J, *Miscellanies upon Various Subjects* (4th edition, 1854)
Bell, Sir Charles KCIE,CMG, *Tibet Past & Present* (OUP, 1925)
Bingley, Revd. W, *Tours round Wales performed during the summer of 1798* (1800)
Bodmer, K., *Karl Bodmer's America*, annotated by David C Hunt & Martha V.Gallagher (University of Nebraska, Lincoln, 1984)
Booz , Elizabeth B, *A Guide to Tibet*, (Collins, 1986)
Burningham, N., 'Notes on the Water Craft of Than Ho Province, N. Vietnam', Int J. Nautical Arch. 229 -238 (1904)
Caesar, 'De Bello Civile', Bk 1 Ch.4
Camden's *Brittania*, translated by E. Gibson (1695)
Catlin, G, *Letters and Notes on the Manners, Customs and Conditions of the North American Indians* (1896)
Chesney, F R, *The Expedition for the Survey of the rivers Euphrates and Tigris* (1853)
Clarke, J H, *Usk Past & Present* (1892)
Collyer, R J, *The Teifi , Scenery and Antiquities of a Welsh river* (Llandysul, 1987)

The Royal Commission to enquire into Salmon Fishing (1863)

The Coracle Society's Newsletters

Craft Tools of Yesterday (Cambs, 1979)

Donovan, E, *Descriptive Excursions through S. Wales & Mons* (1805)

English Pamphlet *Witches & Witchcraft* (1613)

Gilbert, H A, *The Tale of a Wye Fisherman* (1929)

Gilman, Carolyn, *The Way to Independence* (St Paul USA, 1987)

Graesser, N, *Advanced Salmon Fishing – Lessons from Experience* (Bury St. Edmunds, 1987)

Greenwood Trust, Interview – Eustace Rogers (1991)

Guest, Lady, *The Mabinogion: a translation* (1887)

Hall, S C Mr and Mrs, *The Book of South Wales, the Wye and the Coast* (Charlotte James Publishers, 1861)

Hayden and Cosson, C, *Sport and Travel in the Highlands of Tibet* (1927)

Heath, C, *Excursions down the Wye* (Monmouth, 1799)

Hibbert, C, *London: the Biography of a City* (London, 1969)

Holinshed – *Last volume of The Chronicles of England, Scotland & Ireland* (1577)

Hornell J, *Water Transport, Origins and Early Evolution* (Cambridge 1946)

Illustrated London News, 3 December 1932

Independent Newspaper, 24 September1987

Ironbridge Gorge Museum: Interviews with the late Eustace Rogers (1982)

Jones, J F, ' Salmon Fisheries 1863' in the Carmarthenshire Antiquary (1962)

Jones-Byford, W, *Severn Valley Stories* (Shropshire Star & Journal Ltd, Wellington)

The Kidderminster Times, 2 June 1972

King, L. Mrs (Rin-Chen-Lha-Mo) *We Tibetans* (1926)

Laird, Thos and Greg Nicholson, Condé Nast Traveller Magazine (1998)

Locke, S, *Classical Boat Magazine* (1989)

Lucas, A.V, *Symbols of the Wye Valley* (1948)

Hornell J, 'Coracles of South India', in *Man*, monthly record of Anthropological Science. p.157 et seq (1933)

Hornell, J, *British Coracles and Irish Curraghs* (1938)

McGrail, Prof. S, *Boats of the World* (Oxford 2001)

McGrail, Prof S, *Ancient Boats in North West Europe* (London, 1987)

Montgomerie, T G, *Report on a Route Survey made from Nepal to Lhasa* (1868)

Mugridge, A J, *Coracles , Miners and other Memories* (1997)

Neil, Wm T, *The Florida Anthropologist*, Vol 7 (1974)

O' Brien, M, Ediphone Recorded Interview by John Delargy, 16 June 1930

Parker, J F Mrs, *Old Bewdley & its Industries*, Worcestershire Archaelogical Soc. (For 1932-Worcester, 1933)

Peel, J H B, *Portrait of the Severn* (London, 1968)

Pennant, T, *Tours in Wales* (London, 1810)

Phillips, J R, *A History of Cilgerran* (1867)

Phillips, P, *The Times*, 7 January 1989

Prasad, B, *The Tigari – a primitive type of boat used in Bengal* (Asiatic Society of Bengal, 1920)

Raven, M, *Shropshire in Pictures* (1997)

Roberts & Shackleton, *The Canoe* (Canada, 1983)

Seton, G, *The Charm of Skye* (1931)

Shaw, David Limburn, *The A-Z of Betws-y-coed* (Llanrwst, 1990)

Shaw, Lachan, the Revd, *History of the Province of Moray* (Edinburgh, 1775)

Smith, S, *A view from the Ironbridge* (Ironbridge Gorge Museum Trust, 1979)

Stevens, E S, Mrs, *By Tigris & Euphrates* (1923)

Simmonds, R. Capt., 'Diary of the Marches of the Royal Army during the Great Civil War', quoted in *Salopia Shreds & Patches*, Vol 119 (Shrewsbury, 1885)

Thesiger, Wilfred, *The Marsh Arabs* (London, 1964)

Waters, B, *Severn Tide* (London, 1947)

Waters, B, *Severn Stream* (1949)

Watkins, Prof T, *Prehistoric Coracles in Fife* (IJNO 9, 1980)

Williams, Tony, *Forgotten People* (Llandysul, 1997)

Wilson, Gilbert L, *Waheenee – an Indian Girl's Story* (unpublished PhD, 1927)

Wyndham, H P, *A Tour through Montgomeryshire & Wales* (1781)

Yarrell, *A History of British Fishes*, Vol 2 (1836)

Further reading

'British Coracles and Irish Currachs' in *Mariners' Mirror,* the Quarterly Journal of the Society for Nautical Research (London, 1938)

Ahler, Stanley et al., *People of the Willows , the Prehistory and early history of the Hidatsa Indians* (University of North Dakota, 1991)

Bradley, A G, *Clear Waters* (Constable & Co Ltd., 1915)

Catlin, G, *Manners, Customs and Conditions of the N. American Indian,* Vols. 1 and 2 (New York, 1841)

Evans, Prof. E E, *Irish Folkways* (Routledge & Keegan Paul, 1957)

Fenton, Alexander, 'The Curragh in Scotland', *Journal of the School of Scottish Studies* (Edinburgh, 1972)

Herodotus, Book 1: *The Histories,* translated by Robin Waterfield (Oxford, 1998)

Hughes-Parry, J, *A Salmon Fisherman's Note Book* (London, 1949)

Jenkins, J. G, *Nets & Coracles* (Newton Abbot 1974)

Shaw-Smith, D, *Ireland's Traditional Crafts* (Thames & Hudson,1984)

Wilson, Gilbert L, *Wahenee, an Indian Girl's Story told by herself* (Lincoln, USA and London, 1927)

Acknowledgements

During the last twenty years or so I have met a great variety of people all over the world who have had one thing in common, namely a deep interest in, and concern for those who make and use, coracles. Everyone, without exception, has been most kind and helpful. To them I express my gratitude.

A number of museums have provided a substantial amount of information. They are too numerous to mention, but I must single out the Museum of Welsh Life, and particularly its current Director, John Williams-Davies, and its former Curator, Dr J Geraint Jenkins.

I am also indebted to Dr Michael Duffy of Exeter University and Professor Emeritus Sean McGrail of Oxford University, who assisted me greatly in helping me to put the results of many years of research into a coherent shape.

Without the Coracle Society and its members my knowledge of coracles would have been much the poorer. To all of them I say 'thank you'. I particularly wish to express my gratitude to the following Vice Presidents and members: Bernard Thomas, Ronald Davies, the late Edgworth Evans, the late Eustace Rogers, the late Jack Davies, John E Davies, traditional coraclemen alll. An immensely knowledgeable coracleman also is Raymond Rees of Carmarthen. He has been unstinting in his advice and provision of information.

Past and present members of the Coracle Society to whom I am particularly grateful are: Major David Goddard, Terry Kenny, Peter Faullkner, Gerwyn Lewis, Charles Fogg, Paul Jones, and Alan and Nina Grove.

I owe a substantial debt of gratitude to Conwy Richards, who has provided me with a bottomless pool of information, without which this book would be much the poorer.

My thanks go to Sue Dunn for typing large sections of my manuscript.

Any book is often only as good as its Editor. In this regard I have been singularly fortunate in having such a charming and skilful Editor as Jen Llywelyn. I marvel at her ability to understand the world of coracles so quickly.

Picture Credits

Unless credited below, photographs are by the author.

State Historical Society, North Dakota (Figs. 1:1, 1:3)
The Ironbridge Gorge Museum Trust (Plate 7)
Paul Jones (Plate 8)
Bewdley Museum (Fig. 2:2)
Museum of Welsh Life (Figs. 2:3, 2:9, 2:11, 4:5, 4:6, 4:11, 4:15)
Bridgnorth Museum (Plate 12)
Shrewsbury Museum (Figs. 2:5, 2:6)
Science Museum, London (Fig. 2:12)
Royal Museum of Scotland (Figs. 3:1, 3:2)
National Museum of Ireland (Fig. 3:3)
T H Mason, plate 102, *Ireland from old photographs*, publ. Batsford,
   London, 1971 (Fig. 3:4)
Pontardulais Archive (Fig. 4:8)
Ceredigion Museum (Plate 33)
Conwy Richards (Plates 29 and 34)
Clwyd Record Office (Fig. 4:10)
Nina Grove (Plate 35)
Graham Crerar (Plate 36)
Raymond Rees (Plate 26)